THE POCKET GUIDE TO
TREES OF BRITAIN
AND
NORTHERN EUROPE

Kyra Brown
71 Elm Bank Gardens
Barnes
London SW13 0NX
England

THE POCKET GUIDE TO
TREES OF BRITAIN
AND
NORTHERN
EUROPE

ALAN MITCHELL

Illustrated by
DAVID MORE

Edited by Pamela Forey

PARKGATE
BOOKS

First published in 1990

This edition published in 1997 by
Parkgate Books Ltd
London House
Great Eastern Wharf
Parkgate Road
London SW11 4NQ
Great Britain

9 8 7 6 5 4 3 2 1

British Library Cataloguing in Publication Data
Mitchell, Alan, 1992-
   The pocket guide to trees of Britain & Northern Europe
   1. Northern Europe. Trees
   I. Title II. More, David
   582.160948

ISBN 1 85585 365 5

Series Design by Dave Allen

Printed in Italy

Contents

Introduction

The British Isles have, at most, about 35 species of tree which are native, and few counties include the natural range of more than twenty of these. The mild, damp climate suits well almost all trees from the temperate world and from Iron Age times until today, trees have been brought here from all parts and some relatively recent introductions spread themselves as if native. The result is that native woodlands are, excepting only some ash, beech and oak woods, monotonous and scrubby. The interesting, fine specimen trees are all in gardens, parks, squares, streets and cemeteries. Around and in any small town there will be some 2–300 species from Chile, North America, North Africa, the Black Sea and Caucasus regions, the Himalaya, Australasia, China, Japan and Korea. Added to these species are another hundred or more cultivars of them and of a few native trees.

It is these trees which are most seen and admired for spectacular displays of flower or autumn colour and imposing stature, and make the city, town and village scene. Another 1200 species can be found in the best parks and gardens. A small book can select only a fraction and must concentrate largely on the most prominent and frequent species and forms. This is helped by excluding as shrubs any species that does not grow to more than 30 ft (9m) on a single stem. A few much less common species and forms are included where these are notable specimens easily found in parks or gardens popular with the public, like Kew, Stourhead and the Royal Parks in London and a few more, less prominent but of exceptional botanical and horticultural interest.

The text leaves out description of features shown in the plates and deals with natural range, history of introduction, rate of growth and size attained and any other noteworthy feature.

BROADLEAVED TREES AND PALMS

Crack & White Willows

The **Crack Willow**, *Salix fragilis*, is native to Britain and is the common lowland waterside willow. It likes to have its roots in streams or rivers rather than in still water, and some of the best stands are in the swampy margins of fast chalk-fed rivers. Large drainage ditches in flood-plains also grow good trees. Left to themselves, Crack Willows grow rapidly, up to 25m in height, with an upright open crown and they have short lives.

In former times willows were pollarded by cutting the stem at 2.5m, and the score or more sprouts that arose were cut every few years for withies and wattle. These trees were very typical of the rural lowland scene. In the present century the practice of pollarding has almost died out and uncut poles have grown into big branches; many have become too heavy for the top of the bole and have broken out.

The trees have a curious method of increase. They shed the slender, brittle-based shoots very easily and these drop into the streams and are borne away; some to come to rest in the slacker waters of muddy bays. There they root quickly and form new trees. Since the trees are either male or female, a stretch of river colonized by a single upstream pioneer tree will have Crack Willows all of the same sex. The pioneer trees arrive by way of the light, fluff-covered, wind-borne seeds.

Crack Willows are easily identifiable by their large glossy green leaves, often hanging in lines from long strong shoots. In winter and early spring the shoots become deep yellow or pale orange, just before the leaves emerge.

male catkin

new leaves

rooting twig

Cricket Bat Willow

Crack Willow

The **White Willow,** *Salix alba*, is probably a native tree but it is more southerly in distribution than the Crack Willow and is only associated with settlements. It is less common, rarely dominates river banks for great distances, but is more often planted in parks and gardens. It grows even faster than the Crack Willow and can exceed 30m in height. Until its early senility sets in, it maintains an acute-topped crown and is highly distinctive with its silvery blue-green leaves. Most trees collapse when their trunks reach one metre in diameter, after about 60 years' growth.

Cricket Bat Willow, 'Coerulea', has the most rapid growth of all. It possesses superior elasticity and resistance to impact, and hence is the wood used for quality cricket bats.

Crack Willow

White Willow

fruiting catkin

fruiting catkin

Crack Willow

White Willow

Weeping Willows

The **Weeping Willow**, *Salix* 'Chrysocoma', was for a long time referred to as the 'Babylon Willow' and is sometimes still listed as *Salix babylonica*. This compounds several errors. No willow is native to the lower Euphrates River and the weeping tree there that caught the eye of the psalmist is a poplar. The Babylon Willow is of Chinese origin, unknown in the wild, a garden form of the Pekin Willow and was taken to the Levant very early, along the ancient silk routes. It was brought from there to Europe before 1730, but remains a tender tree, and no large tree has been known within living memory in Britain, although it is common in the eastern United States from Philadelphia southwards.

The Weeping Willow in Britain is a hybrid between the Babylon Willow and the native White Willow (or perhaps a weeping form of the Golden Willow variant of the White Willow). It is common in parks and gardens throughout England but finds the summers in the north and in Scotland a little cool, and the best growth is in the south. The shoots are yellow, becoming brighter after the New Year and at their best in March, when the leaf-buds are unfolding bright green. The catkins open with the leaves and are sometimes mixed male and female. Entirely female trees are less pendulous and are an older form, *Salix alba* 'Tristis'. In some years trees are attacked by the fungus 'anthracnose of willows' (*Marssonina*) and lose much of their foliage, although they rarely die.

The **Sallow,** *Salix caprea,* is native to all parts of Britain. It grows to its biggest size, up to 20m tall, in the high rainfall of the western Highlands of Scotland in woods of oak and tussock grass on wet boulder-strewn soils, but it also springs up on waste ground in dry areas to make a tall bush. The majority of the silver-haired,

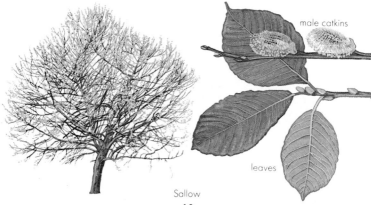

male catkins

leaves

Sallow

egg-shaped catkins open between February and mid April. The males have golden anthers and are the familiar 'pussy willow'. The females have green projecting styles and secrete nectar, so the plants are pollinated by insects as well as by wind-blown pollen. Female trees produce fluffy seeds, like white cotton wool, in June.

male flowers

Weeping Willow

leaves

Weeping Willow in spring

Weeping Willow in summer

White Poplars

The group of poplars known as White Poplars is distinguished from other poplars in having the shoots and the undersides of the leaves thickly covered in white woolly hairs. They are also distinguished from Black and Balsam Poplars by having catkin-scales fringed with long hairs.

The **Aspen**, *Populus tremula*, is native to Britain but is only common in the Scottish Highlands where it grows beside streams and rivers. It differs from the other white poplars in that its leaves have the same unlobed shape on vigorous young shoots as on old wood and they soon shed their hairs. In southern England Aspens are local, making thickets here and there at the edges of woods on damp, low-lying ground. These thickets usually consist of trees of one sex, suggesting that they have been formed by suckers from a single original tree. Suckers arise in well-spaced dense groups extending 10m or more, beyond and within the thickets. Male trees bear catkins, opening brown with pale grey fluffy hairs before March. Female trees bear copious seeds.

The **White Poplar**, *Populus alba*, is a much less robust or common tree than the Grey Poplar in Britain, and comes from southern Europe, northern Africa and western Asia. It is sometimes seen growing as an inland defence against blown sand behind sand dunes or in hedges. It is short-lived and seldom as much as 25m

Grey Poplar

leaf

underside of leaf

female catkins

male catkins

Grey Poplar

tall, but can be spectacular in sunshine; the undersides of its leaves are stark white and show up well against a blue sky. When they are newly out of bud only the undersides show and the crown is a cloud of silvery specks.

The **Grey Poplar**, *Populus canescens*, is intermediate in most features between the Aspen and the White Poplar but is very much more vigorous than either. It is probably a hybrid between them. It grows to a great size and must have a life span of over 200 years, with an extraordinary resistance to wind and a high tolerance of soil conditions. It grows best in broad valleys in chalk or limestone areas. It would make a good replacement for the elms which have much the same needs and stature, but it has an extensive superficial root system and suckers freely; farmers dislike it. It is often mistaken for the White Poplar, but it is very different in its big sturdy trunk and strong heavy branches rising to make multiple-dome crowns, and the foliage is considerably less pure white.

Aspen

White Poplar

leaves

leaves

fruiting catkin

leaf underside

bark

Aspen

White Poplar

Black & Balsam Poplars

The native **Black Poplar**, *Populus nigra* var. *betulifolia*, is a fine tree that has become scarce in the countryside, replaced in lowland valleys by the hybrid Black Italian Poplar which grows more rapidly and, being a male tree, does not strew the area with cotton wool seeds in summer. However the native tree is remarkably resistant to the smoky air once normal in cities, and a male form was widely planted under the name 'Manchester Poplar'; it is still common in cities and suburbs.

The **Lombardy Poplar**, *Populus nigra* 'Italica', is an upright, narrow form of the southern European Black Poplar. It arose in northern Italy and was brought to Britain in 1758. The true form is a male tree and bears numerous dark red catkins. The tapering crown leads the eye upwards and seems to be taller than it actually is. In towns, the Lombardies are often lopped to some 12m, on the grounds of safety, but in fact if left alone the trees resist windthrow very well until they die, and they regrow to over 30m within 15 years. However they now have six tops instead of one; these may destabilize the tree and are also likely to be blown out.

The **Western Balsam Poplar**, *Populus trichocarpa*, is the common Balsam throughout Britain, introduced from the western United States. It is often planted in gardens for the sweet balsam scent of its expanding buds and new spring foliage, but it is usually regretted when, after five years, it is as tall as the house and its suckers have taken over the garden. It is distinctive for the white undersides of its leaves and their very varied size. Male trees bear big thick catkins which become dull red before the leaves unfold. Females have green catkins which ripen into fluff-covered seeds, shed in May.

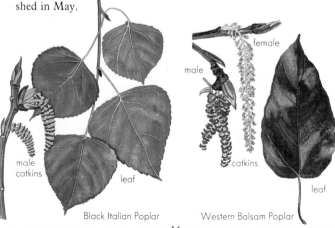

Black Italian Poplar   Western Balsam Poplar

The **Black Italian Poplar,** *Populus* 'Serotina', was the first of a number of hybrids to arise in European nurseries between the European Black Poplar, *Populus nigra*, and the American Eastern Cottonwood, *Populus deltoides*. It is the common big poplar in the chalk valleys of southern England and was also planted in city parks; today it is rarely planted in cities because it matures rapidly into a huge open tree with heavy branches likely to be shed. This is the last countryside tree to come into leaf, in late May, but at least six weeks before that it opens dark red male catkins. The leaves unfold dark orange-brown, paling in a week or so to grey-green.

Black Poplar

male catkins

female catkins
with fruit

Black Poplar

Lombardy Poplar

Walnuts

The name 'Walnut' comes from the Anglo-Saxon for 'foreign nut', and so was in use before the Norman Conquest, probably dating from Roman times. It may refer to the fruit rather than the tree but the **Common Walnut**, *Juglans regia*, has been grown in Britain for a very long time. The Romans associated their god Jupiter (Jove) with this tree, hence the Latin name *juglans*, 'Jove's acorn (*glans*) or nut'. To the Americans it is the 'English' or 'Persian' Walnut as opposed to their several native species. The latter name puts it within its natural range, which is from China and central Asia through Iran and Asia Minor to the Balkan Mountains, but north and west from there is present only from early, unrecorded plantings. It is common in Britain only in southern and central England north to eastern Yorkshire, where there are many beside roads in farmland, but quite large trees are found in parks and gardens north to Skye in the west and to Easter Ross.

Walnuts need deep, fertile, well-drained but moist soils, to grow well. The unfolding leaves are frost tender but expand late enough to avoid most frosts. Walnuts also need long hot summers for the fruits to ripen and British trees usually only produce green fruits, suitable for pickling. Trees are rarely planted in Britain therefore for their nut crop but they do merit planting for their handsome foliage, whitish-grey bark and picturesque aspect. They are frequent in parks and gardens and grow fast, reaching 23m in

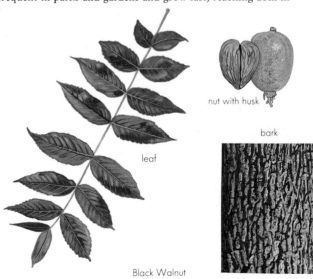

nut with husk

bark

leaf

Black Walnut

height. The trees are short-lived but few are left to become senile in any event, because the wood is so valuable.

Black Walnut, *Juglans nigra*, is so-called because it has dark, scaly and ridged bark even when the trunk is only a few years old. It comes from the Appalachian region in the United States. In Britain it is almost confined to the area southeast of a line from Lincoln to Exeter.

The wood is like that of Common Walnut and both are unsurpassed for use as gunstocks because, once seasoned and worked, neither moves at all and they withstand shock particularly well. They are also valued in furniture for their good colour and their ability to take a high polish.

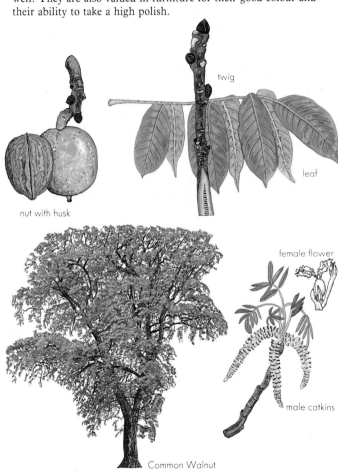

twig

leaf

nut with husk

female flower

male catkins

Common Walnut

Birches

There are two different species of birch native to Britain, both of them widespread and commonly called 'silver birch'. To most people that is the end of the matter, but in fact the two are quite distinct when looked at closely. Even from a distance, the weeping outer crown and the black diamond shapes on the bark proclaim the true species.

The true **Silver Birch**, *Betula pendula*, is the one common on the dry parts of heaths, in open woods on sands and gravels and on the quick-draining slopes of mountain glens. It is a pioneer species and is the first tree to appear on cleared, burned or disturbed land on open soils. Its light seeds are blown far from woodlands. Dense drifts of birch on many southern heaths mark the passage of past fires. The trees grow quickly when young and attain a height of 20m in 25 years, but after that growth slows down and few trees reach 25m. They are short-lived, showing signs of age once they are 60 years old.

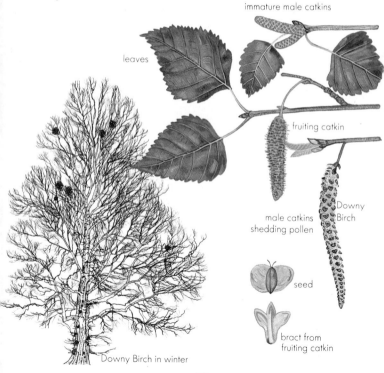

immature male catkins

leaves

fruiting catkin

male catkins shedding pollen

Downy Birch

seed

bract from fruiting catkin

Downy Birch in winter

The tree is always shedding something. In spring it is the bud-scales coming down like chaff, then the male catkins, and after them all summer it deposits systems of dead twigs, as it may too in winter. There is then a long period during which the seeds float down by the million, helped by the redpolls, siskins and tits for which this tree is a main source of autumn food. Then the remains of the fruits come down. On loamy soils this tree makes an ideal lightly shading tree for many rhododendrons and in spring it gives enough light to suit most bulbs. But on poor sandy soils its roots are too invasive and competitive for any but tough plants.

Downy Birch, *Betula pubescens*, is the other tree commonly known as 'silver birch'. It replaces it in damp hollows on heaths, by streams and pools in open woodland and by ditches and streams along the bottom of highland glens, where its fuzzy outline contrasts with that of the weeping Silver Birch above it. It occurs frequently in town and city parks on clay soils and is similar to the Silver Birch in the sizes and ages that it achieves.

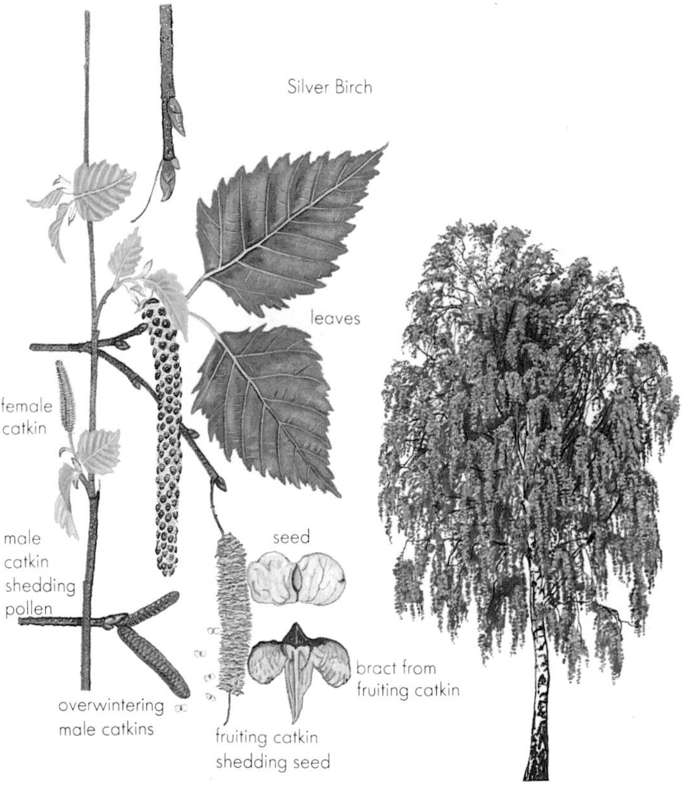

Silver Birch

leaves

female catkin

male catkin shedding pollen

seed

overwintering male catkins

fruiting catkin shedding seed

bract from fruiting catkin

Alders

Common Alder, *Alnus glutinosa*, is a native of Britain found mainly by still or running water. It is able to grow on wet and often flooded sites, and on soils lacking in nitrates, because its roots have nodules which harbour a bacterium capable of extracting nitrogen from the air. It is thus a valuable pioneer species, improving new soils for other trees.

The alder was formerly valued for its timber, used where continual wetting and drying soon rot most woods, for example in mill-clogs and canal-gates, as well as for high quality charcoal. For this last and other smallwood produce, its strong coppicing ability is a great asset. Sprouts from an alder root system can grow 1.3m or more in a season. The dense bunches of dark red roots, that this tree puts into adjacent fresh water, were at one time valued for the way they defend mud-banks against erosion from floodwater and the wash from passing craft.

Common Alder has dark green summer foliage and is rarely used as an ornamental tree, the leaves even fall green in autumn. The flowering of the male catkins is a protracted event, occurring from January to April.

Grey Alder, *Alnus incana*, is a tough and hardy tree from northern Europe which, far from needing a wet site, grows best in well-drained soil and even thrives in the often dry and difficult soils of spoil tips. It also grows well in broken, rocky soils in high rainfall areas, and is to be seen in car parks and public places in the western Highlands of Scotland. Maturing trees are notable for their

Grey Alder

leaves

male catkins

female catkins

opened fruits in winter

Grey Alder in winter

smooth, pale grey-green bark. In autumn the leaves stay on the tree until late November, turning black as they are shed.

Italian Alder, *Alnus cordata*, comes from Corsica and southern Italy. This is the aristocrat of the commonly seen alders, the finest in foliage and the champion in stature and size of fruits. The male catkins become bright yellow and open with the first of the Common Alder, but they are much longer and more impressive. However they all flower within a few weeks. The crown maintains a good conical shape until the tree is 20m or more tall, which added to its other good features, makes this a good tree for precincts and roadsides.

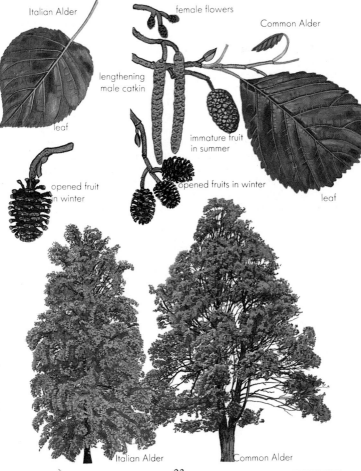

Italian Alder

female flowers

Common Alder

lengthening
male catkin

leaf

immature fruit
in summer

opened fruit
in winter

opened fruits in winter

leaf

Italian Alder

Common Alder

Hornbeams & Hazel

Common Hornbeam, *Carpinus betulus*, is a native tree found mainly in southeast England. The name 'Hornbeam' means 'hard wood'. It is one of the hardest and strongest of all timbers and is a good fuel-wood, also making high quality charcoal. It is still used today for piano hammers, and larger pieces form the centres of chopping blocks. Before the invention of cast iron, hornbeam was the one wood strong and hard enough to take the strain of a watermill wheel and the wear of its cog-teeth. It was also used for the hubs of cartwheels.

Hornbeam grows better than all but a few trees on heavy clays, a useful feature for a tree whose main population is on the London clays of Essex and Hertfordshire. It grows well on lighter soils but not on poor acid sands and it needs sheltered conditions. The male catkins, which are inside buds in the winter (unlike those of hop-hornbeams) expand before the leaves in March and April.

European Hop-hornbeam, *Ostrya carpinifolia*, is a sturdy scaly-barked tree, sometimes with several stems, and quite vigorous, although none is very big in Britain. It is infrequent and most easily spotted in summer, when the fruits hang white among dark, rather flaccid leaves. The male catkins are exposed from autumn to spring, in small bunches like those of alders and hazels, and lengthen to shed pollen in March or April. This tree is wild and quite common across southern Europe from eastern France to the Black Sea and in Asia Minor.

Hazel, *Corylus avellana*, is found everywhere in the British Isles except in the Shetlands. It is not officially a tree, as it fails to

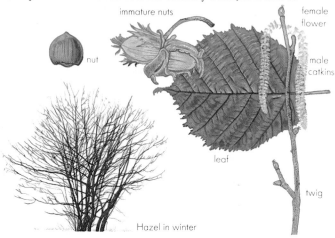

immature nuts

female flower

nut

male catkins

leaf

twig

Hazel in winter

achieve 6m on a single stem, although some bushes may be taller than that. Its strong sprouting growth when cut makes it ideal for coppiced growth under clean-boled oaks. This kind of woodland management, 'coppice with standards', was widespread in the woods of southern England until this century. The periodic clearing of each area encouraged a rich growth of bluebells and also favoured nightingales, so some woods are managed like this today, for conservation. The hazel wood was used for turnery and tool-handles, and its supple shoots were woven into hurdles. In most seasons the catkins appear between late January and April.

European
Hop-hornbeam

bark

leaf

fruit cluster

female
flower

leaf

Hornbeam

male
catkins

twig

fruit cluster

Beech

No tree can grow up under the shade of its own kind, but the **Beech**, *Fagus sylvatica*, can do so under any native tree except Yew. Hence, in time, all areas with suitable soils left undisturbed would become beechwoods. Beech, however, will not grow on heavy clay or other wet soils, but must have open, well-drained soils, so the clay vales and river bottoms would become oakwoods. Beech dominates on chalk and limestone uplands and on mildly acid sands. Its roots penetrate far through open soils and chalk rock, but often do not penetrate deeply, so old beech trees are often blown over, exposing root plates of great extent but no depth.

Adapted to starting life in existing woodland, Beech cannot start life on its own in exposed open ground. When trees are planted for shelter belts or in plantations, they are planted with trees, like Scots Pine, Larch, Lawson Cypress or Sycamore as 'nurse trees' to provide shade and suppress grass cover. The nurse trees are cut when saleable. Once established Beech resists exposure very well and is an invaluable shelter tree in upland areas. Trees survive for up to 200 years and grow up to 40m tall.

A curious feature of the Beech is the 'juvenile cone', a zone about 2m broad at the base, tapering to an end 2.5m high, within which the foliage looks the same as the adult but remains in winter rich red-brown on the tree. Beech hedges are cut to remain within this zone and where clipping is neglected and shoots project beyond it, the part beyond sheds its leaves. Similarly, sprouts on the boles of old trees retain their leaves where they are within this zone.

Copper Beech

Beech in autumn

The **Copper Beech**, 'Purpurea', was first known in Switzerland by 1680, and also arose twice later in Germany. The name is a general, if seldom apt one applied to an array of forms. Superior forms like 'Swat Magret' and 'River's Purple' have a good deep red colour. Growth of Copper Beeches is as rapid as that of the green.

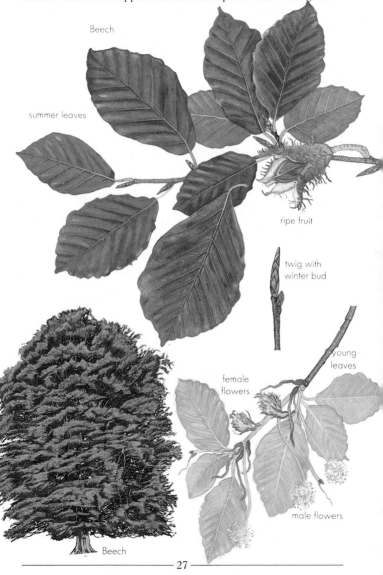

Beech

summer leaves

ripe fruit

twig with winter bud

young leaves

female flowers

male flowers

Beech

Sweet Chestnut

The **Sweet Chestnut**, *Castanea sativa*, is a tree from southern Europe that may have been introduced by the Romans. They certainly brought the nuts to eat, but the tree may not have been grown in Britain until much later. It has, in any case, been established in Britain since very early times and behaves as if it were native. It grows far into northern Scotland, but grows much faster and bigger in southern England and Ireland, reaching 35m in height with boles over 10m round.

Older trees have prominently spiralled bark. Until they are about 50 years old or 60cm through, the boles have few fissures and these tend to be straight. From then on fissures divide into more and more shallow ridges and lean into a spiral. When the bole measures about one metre through, the tree has the ridges in a marked spiral only a little out of the vertical, but by the time it is 2m through, the spiral is at about 45° and it flattens further with greater age.

The arrangement of the sexes of the flowers is odd. The first to open are the numerous male catkins from the buds behind the shoot tips. They are joined by the females – little, brilliant green rosettes with white styles – from buds at the tips of the shoots and sometimes on little branches of their own, but usually at the bases of some short catkins which are not open. Weeks later these may open as male flowers and stand up as spikes of flower with a completely different aspect from the earlier males. In good years the nuts will enlarge and ripen to be comparable with imported nuts for dessert, but in most years the cool summers make them of little use for this purpose.

The timber of Sweet Chestnut has most of the good features of that of oak, but lacks the figure in the grain. The trees also have

leaf

fruit

husk with fruit

Sweet Chestnut

the habit of yielding 'shaken' timber, either from the felling impact or from 'shakes' already there. These are cracks which render the wood worthless for any but the smallest uses. Sweet Chestnut makes an excellent coppice, the stools being cut every 15 years or so and the wood being used for palings and hop-poles; the coppiced woods are rich in bluebells and insects and some such woods are still worked as conservation areas today.

Sweet Chestnut

female flowers

leaves

male catkins

twig

Sweet Chestnut

winter tree

Oaks

The **English Oak**, *Quercus robur*, ranges across the plains of
northern Europe to the eastern lowlands of Britain, leaving the west
and mountains largely to the Sessile Oak. It grows best on damp,
heavy clays but will grow on sandy soils. It is a singularly robust
tree and remains in full health while its leaves, flowers, fruits and
roots nourish a vast array of insects, including many gall wasps.
These festoon the trees in often colourful galls like cherries,
currants, apples, and one like the hop fruit, while a recent addition
causes hideous distortion to acorns. The bark may carry ferns,
mosses and lichens, while dead branches support many fungi and
larvae of beetles and moths. The open pattern of the woods formed
by this oak allow many other trees and shrubs to grow.

In former times oaks were often cut back when quite young, at
about 2.5m. Trees pollarded like this sprouted new branches out of
the reach of browsing deer, but many have been left uncut for the
last 150 years or more, and such trees have now made hugely
spreading crowns. The acorns grow in pairs on 4–8cm long stalks;
the leaves are practically stalkless with an auricle at the base.

The **Sessile Oak**, *Quercus petraea*, is dominant in high rainfall
areas with light soils. The bole tends to be straight with a head of
radiating straight branches at about 5–10m. The evenly spread
foliage casts more shade than that of Common Oak and few other

Sessile Oak

leaf

acorn

trees or tall shrubs grow in Sessile Oak woods. They are however, for this reason, the homes of Pied Flycatchers and Redstarts which have the space to feed beneath the crowns. The leaves are firm and solid, free of galls, symmetrically lobed and with long yellow stalks. The acorns are stalkless.

The **Downy Oak**, *Quercus pubescens*, has short, quite dense down all over its shoots, leaves and leaf stalks. It is the common oak on dry hillsides from Spain eastwards across southern Europe. From a distance it looks just like a Common Oak with darker, duller foliage and is rare in Britain.

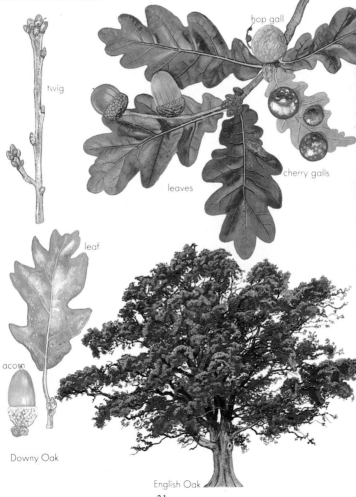

twig

hop gall

leaves

cherry galls

leaf

acorn

Downy Oak

English Oak

Oaks

The **Turkey Oak**, *Quercus cerris*, is a tree of southern Europe, found from France to Romania. It was introduced into Britain in 1735 but behaves as if has always been there. Like the Sweet Chestnut it seeds itself freely in the south of England on light soils and grows very well far into the northeast of Scotland, although its growth is less rapid there than in the south. The biggest tend to be in Devon and Sussex.

Growth of this tree is very rapid, and the oak makes a fine straight bole from its early years. Timbermen are however unimpressed by the fine boles of Turkey Oaks because they are usually flawed by 'shakes' – serious internal cracking. Although the tree colours well in autumn, when it may be a rich orange-brown, it is dark foliaged and dull all summer.

The **Cork Oak**, *Quercus suber*, is all too often an inordinately dull, bushy plant with a tendency to rest big low branches on the ground. Only a few in Cornwall are respectable specimen trees. The tree comes from the Mediterranean region but is hardy in the north of Scotland. Where it grows in Spain and Portugal, the very thick, deeply fissured, often pale cream bark is stripped away for its cork every few years.

leaf

underside of leaf

acorn

bark

Cork Oak

The **Holm Oak**, *Quercus ilex*, derives its English name from an old word 'holm', meaning holly. It has hard, spine-toothed, holly-like leaves while it is young and its foliage is at hazard from grazing. Like the holly itself, its adult leaves are untoothed, unspined and unlobed. It has a dark, uninspiring aspect with a general effect of unchanging gloom throughout the year, even though its newly unfolded adult leaves are white all over. The undersides of the adult leaves remain covered in white down, like the shoots.

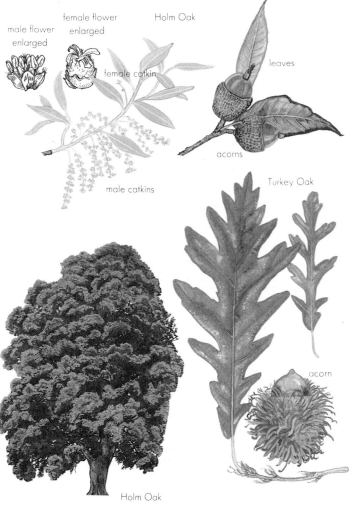

male flower enlarged

female flower enlarged

Holm Oak

female catkin

leaves

acorns

male catkins

Turkey Oak

acorn

Holm Oak

Elms

There is grave doubt whether the **English Elm**, *Ulmus procera*, is in fact English at all, in the sense of being a native tree. There is evidence to suggest that its distribution is linked with the spread of certain tribes before the Iron Age. It almost never sets seed, spreads by root suckers, and it was used both for cattle forage and for marking boundaries.

Before the onset of Dutch Elm Disease the English Elm dominated great tracts of the English landscape, creating a unique rural scene, notably on the eastward slopes of the Cotswolds, in the vale of Aylesbury and along the south coast from Dorset to east Sussex. It was not found to the east of Canterbury which was Smoothleaf Elm country, it faded out north of York, entered Wales only in the Usk valley and in the far south, and was not found west of the A386 in Devon. Today it remains only on the coast in eastern Sussex.

There are two species of Elm Bark beetle which carry the fungal Dutch Elm Disease in England and one of them extends into Scotland. The disease is not Dutch in origin but probably central Asiatic and the Dutch are associated with it only in that they studied it and raised elms with resistance to it. Unfortunately although the hybrids selected resisted the form of the disease then prevalent, they failed in the face of the virulent strain, imported from Canada in about 1965. The new strain can grow through the new wood of the summer growth of the elm shoots, unlike the old strain which was restricted by it, and can move down the trunk and into the root systems which often interconnect along much of a hedgerow. By this means the disease passes from tree to tree without help from the beetles.

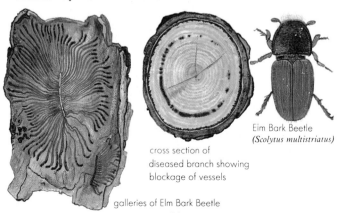

cross section of
diseased branch showing
blockage of vessels

Elm Bark Beetle
(*Scolytus multistriatus*)

galleries of Elm Bark Beetle

The **Smoothleaf Elm**, *Ulmus carpinifolia*, is the common Field Elm of Europe, but its status in Britain is a matter of dispute; it may be native but there is evidence that it also may have been introduced by pre-Iron Age tribes. Few trees have survived Dutch Elm Disease. Before the disease struck, hugely domed trees with boles over 2m in diameter, were found as far west as Gloucestershire. This elm is very late to unfold its leaves and is bare for six weeks or more after the English Elms are in full leaf, but its red flowers open at much the same time in late February or early March. It has many basal sprouts and shoots grow from bosses on the bole.

leaf

fruit

Smoothleaf Elm

fruit

flowering shoot

leaves

English Elm

Elms

The **Wych Elm**, *Ulmus glabra*, is an undisputed native of the British Isles, whatever views may be held about the English Elm. It is common in hillside woods in the Highlands of Scotland wherever it is shady and damp, and on higher ground amongst boulders by streamsides in Scotland, Cumbria and the Pennines. In the south the Wych Elm was much less common even before all the big trees were killed by Dutch Elm Disease. It grew locally in damp woods and parklands. In the north and in Scotland it is planted in city parks and is one of the most resistant trees to smoky city air.

It has smooth, pale grey bark, densely hairy shoots and leaf stalks and exceptionally hairy leaves which feel rather like sandpaper. The flowers open, pressed close to the shoots, in February or March and the fruits are fully developed and prominent in apple green bunches well before the leaves unfold, bright green and pleated. In June the fruits turn pale brown and they fall in July, to lie thick on the ground in many Scottish woods.

The **Dutch Elm**, *Ulmus* x *hollandica* 'Hollandica', is one of a group of hybrids between the Wych and Smoothleaf Elms that have arisen in many places. Its origin is very doubtful and, although valued for its easily worked timber and rapid growth, it was very restricted in distribution, largely in the region now devoid of elms. Its bark is unlike that of other elms, being finely flaky and red-brown and the leaves are dark and coarse, leathery and almost smooth on top. It has a distinctive sparse crown, like a flat-topped umbrella.

The **Huntingdon Elm**, *Ulmus* x *hollandica* 'Vegeta', arose in 1760 when seed was collected from a fine Smoothleaf Elm standing near a Wych Elm, by the Huntingdon nurserymen, Ingram and Wood. It is very distinct in its crown, with a high dome held on strong, straight, radiating branches and is a good avenue tree, much

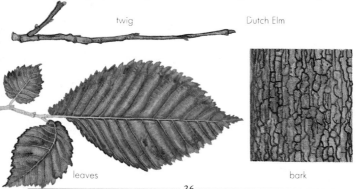

twig

Dutch Elm

leaves

bark

planted in city squares and parks. It has smooth leathery leaves and big, pale green sterile fruits.

The **White Elm**, *Ulmus laevis*, from Europe has fruits with a fringe of white hairs like the American Elm, which it also resembles in foliage and in the vase-shaped crown of arching branches.

twig

flowers

immature fruits in April

mature fruit

leaf

Wych Elm   Huntingdon Elm in winter

Zelkova & Nettletrees

The **Caucasus Zelkova**, *Zelkova carpinifolia*, is often called the Caucasian Elm, and is from a distinct group of trees closely related to the true elms. The tree grows wild in the Elburz and Caucasus Mountains and there it has a normal tree form. However when planted in Britain it often looks like a giant erect bush on a short stout trunk. It is hard to see how this form can be a selected cultivar, for the original five trees, believed to be from seed probably imported via France in 1760, are of this form, and so are the biggest and oldest of the other specimens in Britain and Ireland.

The deeply fluted bole, usually 1 – 2m long, but sometimes scarcely that, holds aloft a tall egg-shaped crown of over 100 almost vertical branches, many of about equal small size. And yet there are several specimens in Britain of normal tree shape with boles of up to 12m and normal numbers of moderately ascending branches. In Hyde Park in London the two kinds are mixed. Young trees are slender and grow slowly for some years before they start to grow rapidly and the bole thickens. The autumn colours are old gold and pale brown. In most years the little nuts are borne in plenty. On many of the old bushy trees some of the interior vertical branches are dead and, unable to fall away, rot slowly where they are.

fruit

Caucasus Zelkova

The **Keaki**, *Zelkova serrata*, from Japan has more elegant foliage than the Caucasus tree, with smooth, well-stalked, long-tapered leaves hanging each side of slightly drooping shoots. The crown is a light open hemisphere with subtle yellow, pink and amber colours in autumn. It is now being planted more frequently in Britain, having long been grown in parks and squares in west London.

The **Southern Nettletree**, *Celtis australis*, comes from southern Europe where it makes a big tree; its impressive smooth grey bole is familiar in cities like Nîmes and Auch in France. It feels the lack of warmth in Britain and is confined to the south where, even then, few are more than bushes. It has long-tapered leaves, rough to the touch and with sharply toothed margins.

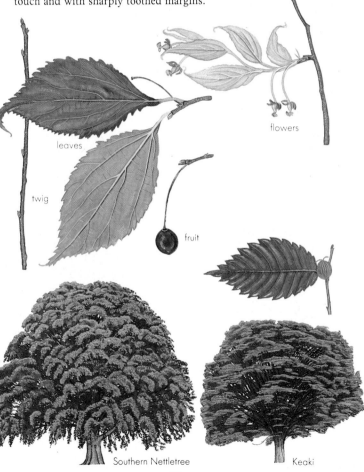

flowers

leaves

twig

fruit

Southern Nettletree

Keaki

Mulberries

The common mulberry in Britain is the **Black Mulberry**, *Morus nigra*, a tree so long known in cultivation and planted so widely that its natural range is unknown beyond the fact that it is Oriental. It must also be of a relatively southern origin because it is common in southern England, rare north of the Midlands as far as Cumbria, and not grown in Scotland. It is prized as an ornamental tree in gardens, grown for its fruit and also for raising silkworms on its foliage. Silkworm caterpillars prefer the White Mulberry but this tree does not grow well in northern climes and the caterpillars will mature and spin cocoons on the Black Mulberry in Britain, although there has been no success in raising them on a large scale.

Black Mulberry starts very slowly from seed and the traditional method of propagation is from 'truncheons'. These are 1.5–2m lengths of branches from an old collapsing tree, and with 1m or so in the ground, they sprout great numbers of shoots around the top cut and from burrs below it. They soon make broad bushy trees and bear fruits within 20 years on warm sites. By then they look old and with decay almost inevitably setting in at the cut where the main branches spring up, they in turn become collapsing old trees. Sometimes they were then mounded up to support the branches, which soon rooted into the soil and the old bole was hidden. The reputation of the mulberry as a very slow, very long-lived tree is derived largely from this method of propagation.

A splendid courtyard tree, the mulberry should not be planted where it overhangs paving, for the fallen ripe fruits make the paths

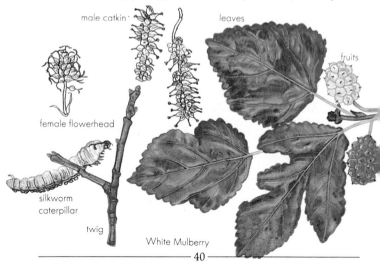

male catkin

leaves

fruits

female flowerhead

silkworm caterpillar

twig

White Mulberry

slippery. The leaves have a glossy surface and a harsh texture from being covered in short, hard hair; those on strong shoots are often deeply and irregularly cut into broad lobes. They turn pale yellow brown in autumn.

The **White Mulberry**, *Morus alba*, is native to China and is the tree upon which the silk industry was founded. It was brought to England in about 1596 but has found no part of the country to its liking and is a bushy, fragile plant given to dying back in the few places where it has been planted.

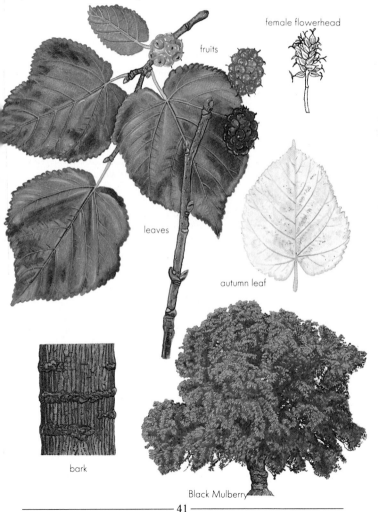

female flowerhead

fruits

leaves

autumn leaf

bark

Black Mulberry

Fig

The **Fig**, *Ficus carica*, has given its name to a huge genus of some 800 members of the Mulberry family, all evergreen and mostly tropical and varying from small climbers to banyan trees. They all have the same strange flowers which are almost entirely enclosed in a cup. Insects are lured into this through the small aperture and there they collect pollen which they take to another flowerhead when they escape. The whole pollinated flowerhead becomes the succulent fruit.

The Common Fig is, however, an ancient selection of a female plant which bears fruit without need for fertilization. This is just as well since the necessary specialized fig wasps do not live in Britain. The tree is native to western Asia and may have been introduced into Britain by the Romans; it is only marginally hardy in this country except in the south and only reliably produces edible fruits if grown against a wall.

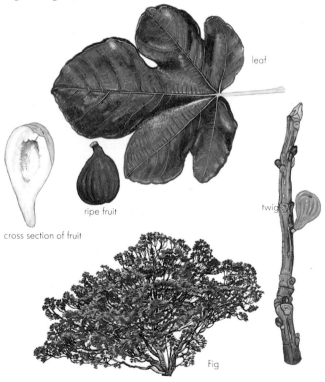

leaf

ripe fruit

twig

cross section of fruit

Fig

Tulip-tree

The **Tulip-tree**, *Liriodendron tulipifera*, belongs to the Magnolia family and has magnolia-like flowers but very different buds and leaves. It is native to the USA and common from New England to Louisiana.

In its native areas it grows with a narrow open crown until 40m tall. Big trees are frequent across England south of the Midlands and in south Wales, but thin out rapidly to the north, to be of moderate size at best in northern England and in southern Scotland. In the south of England the trees flower after about 25 years but the blooms are largely hidden in the July foliage, and leave unsightly brown seed heads through the winter. It is as a foliage tree that this species excels. In autumn, the leaves turn splendidly gold and pale orange. The wood of the tulip-tree is the soft, even-grained whitewood with which intending joiners learn their skills.

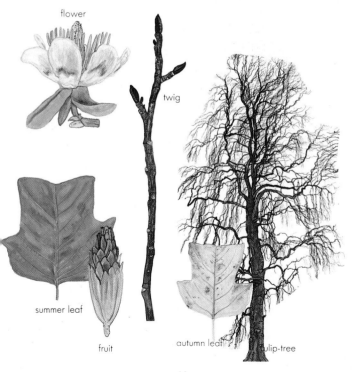

flower

twig

summer leaf

fruit

autumn leaf

tulip-tree

Magnolias

The Magnolias have the most primitive flowers of all the non-conifers: the segments are not divided into distinguishable sepals and petals but are graded from smaller in outer rows to bigger in the inner whorls, and are all classed as 'tepals', a handy anagram. Those prominent in spring with flowers on bare wood are Asiatic whereas all the American species flower when in full leaf.

The **Saucer Magnolia**, *Magnolia* x *soulangiana*, is the popular front-garden magnolia, broad and bushy and full of flower. It is a hybrid between the Chinese Yulan, *Magnolia denudata* and a Japanese species. It has given numerous variants, a few with pure white flowers but most with flowers tinged with purple or deep red. Among the best is 'Lennei' with bigger darker leaves and a white interior to each rosy-purple tepal. This variety also bears a few flowers throughout the summer.

Campbell's Magnolia, *Magnolia campbelli*, is regarded by some as the queen of the genus and, in the Himalayas when 45m tall and covered in huge rosy-pink flowers, it must be spectacular. In southern and western gardens, when a broad tree to over 18m tall, it also makes its mark. In normal years the flowers open between mid-February and late March. Once the big hairy bud scales have

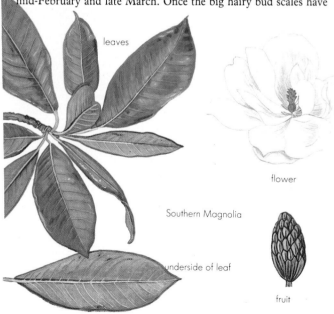

leaves

flower

Southern Magnolia

underside of leaf

fruit

parted, the flowers are likely to be killed by frost, so a period without any frost must follow any early warm spell for there to be any display. In mid-flower the outer eight to twelve tepals droop leaving the inner four erect. It takes about 25 years growth from seed before the tree produces any flowers. The white flowered form 'Alba' grows more strongly.

The **Southern Magnolia** or Evergreen Magnolia, *Magnolia grandiflora*, is native to the USA, from North Carolina to Texas. It is a favourite plant for the south-facing wall of an English mansion and is seen free-standing, up to 12m tall, only south and west of the Thames. The sweetly scented flowers open from midsummer onwards, and may measure 25cm across.

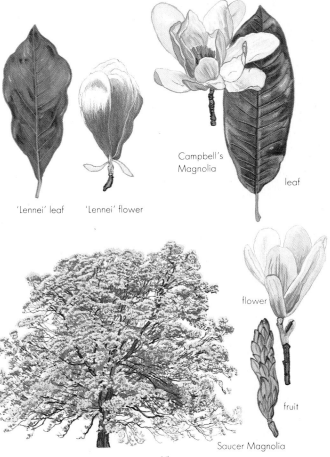

'Lennei' leaf   'Lennei' flower

Campbell's
Magnolia

leaf

flower

fruit

Saucer Magnolia

Planes

The **London Plane,** *Platanus* x *acerifolia*, was a source of puzzlement for 250 years until in 1919 it was shown to be a hybrid between the Oriental Plane and the American Plane. As well as being intermediate between the parents in depth of lobing on the leaves and in the numbers of fruits on each stalk, the tree shows hybrid vigour to a high degree. This is really the secret of its success in cities, for it has an extremely robust root system which can grow in poor rubble-filled soils, and hard shiny leaves which quickly wash clear of soot and which remain on the tree for only a short season. However, it often grows too large for the confined courts and squares where it is planted in paving; then complaints arise about it blocking the light, lifting paving and shedding slippery leaves. Further, the fine hairs its leaves shed in summer, as well as those from its seeds, break into minute fragments which are carried by the wind and cause irritation to the eyes of some people.

Hybrid vigour may also confer good health, and until recent and local outbreaks of plane-tree anthracnose which kills new shoots and flowers in some seasons but does no serious harm, the tree was free of disease. Since dead planes or planes dropping branches are almost, if not quite, unknown and the oldest are still growing fast, this will increasingly be the biggest British broadleaf tree. The largest are about 50m tall and they grow in the south. Its stature falls away sharply towards the north and it makes a small, untroublesome tree for Glasgow and Edinburgh.

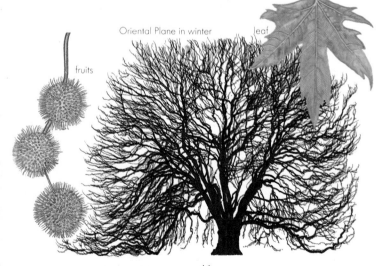

fruits

Oriental Plane in winter

leaf

'Pyramidalis' is the form common in the streets of London and other cities, with a brown burry bark, small three-lobed, bright shiny green leaves and one or two big fruit balls. None of the big trees is of this form, known since 1850.

The **Oriental Plane**, *Platanus orientalis*, has a tendency to grow huge low branches and to rest them on the ground 10m or more away, so it is even less suitable for street planting than the London Plane. It seems to be rather less sensitive to cool summers than that tree, and there are sizable trees in Cumbria and Tayside, but it is much less widely planted everywhere in Britain. The biggest trees are over 25m tall.

London Plane

leaf

new leaves

male flowers

fruits

seed

female flowers

Hawthorns

The **Hawthorn** or May, *Crataegus monogyna*, is a native species seen at its best as a tall, broad bush clothed to the ground on chalk downlands or sandy commons. In this state it covers itself all over with flowers and scents the air during mid-May. It provides birds, especially redwings and fieldfares, with great quantities of dark red berries in October and after. When berries are left in December or January they may attract waxwings.

Hawthorns are also seen as genuine trees, in parks and gardens, where the species is valued for its all-round toughness, growing in poor soils, dry places and polluted air and with branches resistant to all but the most determined vandal. They may then reach 12m in height. By far the greater number of hawthorns, however, are in hedges bounding fields, and most of these are clipped and so lose most of their flowering wood. Easily raised from cuttings, robust when transplanted, clipped into low, thorny, cattle-proof barriers, this was the obvious plant for the big hedge-planting era of the Enclosures after 1820. The timber is very hard and an excellent fuel, burning slowly and hot with a lilac flame.

The **Midland Thorn**, *Crataegus oxyacantha* or *C. laevigata*, prefers the shade of woods on heavy soils, but hybrids between this species and the May are common, despite their different habitats. In the wild, pink-flowered variants are common and they are often planted in suburban parks and gardens. The best is Paul's Scarlet Thorn, with truly red flowers.

The **Plumleaf Thorn**, *Crataegus x prunifolia*, has a few purple thorns and broad dark glossy leaves. It is often mistaken for the

fruits

Midland Hawthorn

Paul's Scarlet Thorn

Cockspur Thorn, an American species rare in Britain, with close rows of long, curved ferocious thorns. The Plumleaf thorn is rugged, free-flowering and fruiting, uniquely coloured in autumn in gold, burnished copper, orange and scarlet, and a splendid tree commonly planted in town parks and gardens and by village roadsides. Unless trained to a single stem, it grows into a low broad bushy tree. The fruits fall with the leaves.

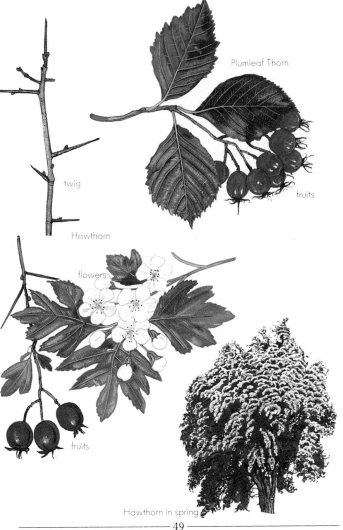

Plumleaf Thorn

twig

fruits

Hawthorn

flowers

fruits

Hawthorn in spring

Rowans & Service Trees

The **Rowan**, *Sorbus aucuparia*, is native throughout Great Britain and Ireland and grows at a higher altitude – over 1000m in Scotland – than any other tree. In the remote north it has the brightest of the autumn leaves, fine orange and scarlet, but where day-length is shorter, as in England where the trees are planted in many town streets and gardens as well as growing wild in open woods, it is at best a mottled orange and dark red and usually the leaves blacken and fall early. The berries turn from green to yellow within a few days in July and then suddenly, within a day or two, they are red and being eaten by blackbirds, thrushes and starlings.

There are many other species and cultivated varieties of Rowans. 'Fastigiata' is narrowly erect and 'Fructolutea' has yellow berries. Scarlet Rowan, *Sorbus* 'Embley', achieves a flaming scarlet in autumn equalled by few trees. It is widely planted in parks and streets (as '*Sorbus discolor*'), but has only recently become common in gardens. The Hupeh Rowan, *Sorbus hupehensis*, comes from western China, but is becoming common in public plantings. It has greyish leaves with red leafstalks, and dull white or sometimes rosy pink berries.

The **Wild Service Tree**, *Sorbus torminalis*, is a native British tree on or near chalk, limestone and clay from Kent to near Carnforth, Cumbria in the west and near Sheffield in the east. It is of particular interest to botanists and ecologists since it will only sow itself in primary woodland, that is on land that has never been cultivated. Its occurrence has been closely studied and mapped and in some woods there is a long history of the tree replacing itself

True Service Tree   globular fruit   pear-shaped fruit

through suckers. It has made several natural hybrids with the Whitebeam.

By contrast, the **True Service Tree**, *Sorbus domestica*, is in a quite isolated group of its own, despite its rowan-like leaves, and it does not hybridise with other species. Even without fruits, it can be told from any rowan, by its ovoid shiny green buds and its rich, dark brown, finely ridged bark. The fruits are big, up to 3cm long, green and brown tinged with red and either globular or pear-shaped.

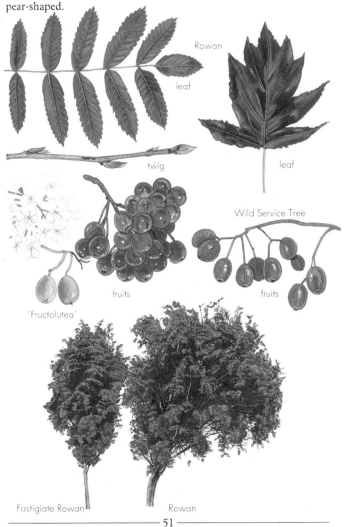

Rowan
leaf
leaf
twig
'Fructolutea'
fruits
Wild Service Tree
fruits
Fastigiate Rowan
Rowan

Whitebeams & Medlar

The **Whitebeam**, *Sorbus aria*, is native to chalk and limestone hills from Kent to the Wye Valley and to County Galway in Ireland. It is planted all over England in gardens, streets and towns but is uncommon in Scotland. It shows up strongly against the dark yews and hollies on the Chilterns, when its leaves emerge brightly silvered and again in autumn when it turns a subtle biscuit-brown, still showing white undersides to the leaves. The berries have usually been eaten by the birds before this and are at their best when ripe in late summer, against the dark green and silver foliage.

The variety 'Lutescens' is usually preferred for streets and small gardens, because it has a neat egg-shaped crown with upswept branches and dark purple shoots against which the unfolding silvery leaf-buds show to advantage.

The **Swedish Whitebeam**, *Sorbus x intermedia*, is one of a series of hybrids which occur in the wild among several species of *Sorbus*, in this case apparently between the Whitebeam and the Rowan. It is very hardy and tough, and is commonly planted in city streets and parks. It can cover itself in flowers almost like a hawthorn and makes a very sturdy tree with a trunk more than 70cm in diameter.

Another complex of these Whitebeam x Rowan hybrids includes the **Finnish Whitebeam** or Bastard Service Tree, *Sorbus x thuringiaca*. It is naturally very upright and compact in crown, but a more strict form is also grown, 'Fastigiata'. They are both planted in car parks and gardens.

The **Medlar**, *Mespilus germanica*, is separable from the closely related thorns, apples and pears by its big solitary flowers and

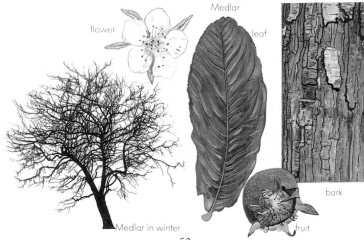

Medlar

flower

leaf

bark

Medlar in winter

fruit

fruits. It was introduced from Europe in very early times to be grown in orchards. The fruits were left on the trees until very ripe in October, and then stored to ripen further until they began to decay, at which point they were, apparently, ready to eat. Although reported to be wild in some Sussex and Kent woods, this tree is not common in gardens. It is most likely to be seen in old gardens associated with cathedrals and abbeys. It is either a bush or has a short trunk and is broader than tall. In autumn the leaves turn a pleasant yellow-brown.

flowers

Finnish Whitebeam

Whitebeam

fruits

fruits

underside of leaf

Swedish Whitebeam

fruits

Whitebeam

Crab Apples

The term Crab Apple, in horticultural use, embraces not just the small-fruited woodland and hedgerow tree but also all the small-fruited non-orchard apples. It includes all the apple trees grown for their flowers or autumn colour — all the exotic species and cultivars grown in gardens. The one garden apple often prized for its fruit and for making into jelly or jam, 'John Downie', is also decorative in fruit; since its fruits are small this is also a Crab Apple.

The **Wild Crab**, *Malus sylvestris*, is a British native tree found scattered in all parts in oakwoods and hedgerows. In one common form it can be told from the 'wild' seedlings arising from discarded cores of domestic apples, which are quite frequent near picnic places and along roads, by its white flowers and thorns. Other forms lack thorns and their flowers are flushed pink; they can be distinguished by their smooth shoots and leaf undersides. The Wild Crab is only one of at least four species that went to make the domestic apple.

The **Hupeh Crab**, *Malus hupehensis*, was found in west China in 1900. It is an outstanding tree in many ways; it grows fast, is very fertile and will not cross with other crabs, the opening flowers are of unsurpassed elegance when in masses on mature trees. The big buds are globular and pale pink, the open flowers are pure white,

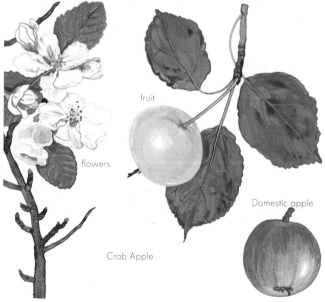

flowers

fruit

Domestic apple

Crab Apple

up to 6cm across with a golden centre and they are followed by many little fruits, bright shining dark red for most of the summer.

The **Japanese Crab**, *Malus floribunda*, is a Japanese hybrid sent to Britain in 1862. It is the commonest crab in suburban gardens and parks, along with some of the Purple Crabs. It comes into leaf very early, before the end of March and by May the leaves are hidden by red buds and pink and white flowers. Every few years there are myriads of tiny yellow fruits.

The **Purple Crab**, *Malus* x *purpurea*, is most acceptable when it first comes into flower. Then the flowers fade badly and the thin purple-stained foliage is borne on branches which grow at awkward angles. Several forms are grown, of which 'Profusion' is the best, with sprays of dark red flowers among dark purple leaves, and persistent dark red fruits.

Hupeh Crab

fruit

flowers

flowers

Japanese Crab

fruit

Purple Crab 'Profusion'

Japanese Crab

Purple Crab 'Profusion'

Pears

The Pears are a small group of Old World trees with white flowers that open before the leaves unfold, and fruits with abundant grit-cells. Their wood is dense, hard and strong and takes a good polish. It is used in turnery and also makes an excellent fuel, burning hot and slowly with a pleasant scent.

The **Common Pear**, *Pyrus communis*, is probably not a native of Britain, at least in the form commonly found. These trees are descendants of naturalized orchard pears, derived originally from hybrids between the Wild Pear and other species from southern Europe. The truly wild form, found in southwestern England, is *Pyrus cordata*, which has little 3cm leaves deeply heart-shaped at the base and globular brown fruits speckled white. The Common Pear is occasionally found wild in hedgerows and at the edges of woods and may be thorny. It is frequently grown in parks and gardens. It has dark brown or black bark, cracked into small, shallow, square plates.

The **Willowleaf Pear**, *Pyrus salicifolia*, grows in the Caucasus region and was introduced to Britain in 1780. It is naturally pendulous in its outer crown and 'Pendula', a low-crowned plant with steeply-arched, weeping branches is seen most frequently. The plant is at its best when the flower buds are nearly ready to open, for each bud is tipped bright red; as they open the white flowers are lost amongst the silvery leaves. In its leafless state, 'Pendula' is unattractive, and in late summer the leaves lose their brightness so this tree is difficult to place, although it is popular in small

Willowleaf Pear

leaves

fruit

flowers

gardens. It looks best overhanging a small pool or as a spring feature against yew hedges.

The **Chanticleer Pear**, *Pyrus calleryana* 'Chanticleer', is the best of all pears, with many merits and a growing popularity. Chanticleer is narrowly erect and is exceedingly tough, robust and vigorous. It is early into flower, often in January, with silvery foliage unfolding before the flowers fade. The leaves are soft grey-green and become shiny, turning yellow, orange, red and crimson in the autumn.

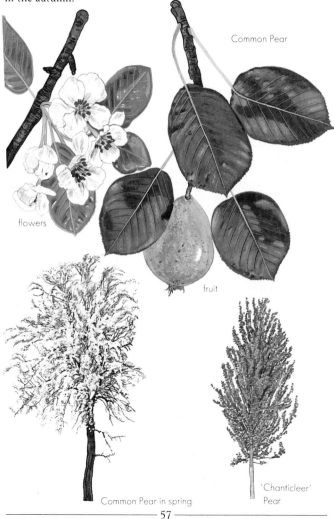

Common Pear

flowers

fruit

Common Pear in spring

'Chanticleer' Pear

Cherry Laurel & Bird Cherry

The **Cherry Laurel,** *Prunus laurocerasus,* is often referred to as just "the Laurel", but it is a Bird Cherry and the true Laurel is in the Bay family. Unlike the leaves of the Bay Laurel which are edible and used in cooking, those of Cherry Laurel contain small amounts of the deadly hydrocyanic acid. It comes from the area south of the Caspian and Black Seas and has been in Britain for over 300 years, taking over large tracts of the country, spreading by seeds, suckers and layers. Nothing else can grow in the shade of its evergreen crown or come up through its heavy, slow-rotting leaf litter. Trees in woods and hillsides, especially on good soils in warm, damp areas, have sometimes perished from its invasion. Its flowerheads are prominent in winter and open in April, when their heady sweet scent travels far. If left to itself this Laurel will grow up to 16m tall, but in parks and gardens it is most commonly seen as a clipped bush, much favoured as a nesting place by song thrushes and blackbirds.

The **Portugal Laurel**, *Prunus lusitanica,* is common as a hedge or as a small tree. In western parts it becomes a larger tree, with smooth or slightly scaling black bark. The very sweetly scented flowers open in mid-June and are numerous on old trees.

The **Bird Cherry,** *Prunus padus,* is native to Scotland, Ireland, Wales, northern England and parts of the Midlands. It is most common by streams high in the Pennines and Cumbria and in Scottish glens. It is very attractive in June, when in flower, and in

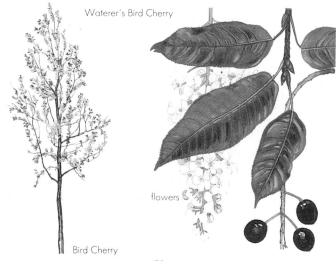

Waterer's Bird Cherry

flowers

Bird Cherry

its soft yellow and amber autumn colours. It is planted in some gardens in the south and sometimes in streets, but it tends to be bushy with more than one stem.

Much more commonly planted is the coarse-growing form, **Waterer's Bird Cherry**, 'Watereri', which can be 18m tall. Its bigger leaves are scattered along whip-like shoots, but it can be a fine sight in flower in good years. The flower-spikes are 15–20cm long and curved.

flowers

Portugal Laurel

fruit

flowers

Cherry Laurel

fruit

Almond, Cherry & Blackthorn

The **Almond**, *Prunus dulcis*, is the first big-flowered tree of the cherry group to open its flowers, which it does several weeks after the opening of the massed little flowers of the Myrobalan Plums, usually in late February. The usual form in parks and gardens is not the one grown for its nuts, which is normally white-flowered, but an old selection or a hybrid with the peach.

Almonds suffer much from the fungus that causes peach-leaf curl, turning leaves bright red and puckered, then brown and black. The fruits hang black and unsightly into the winter. The tree is often short-lived and the best displays of flowers are likely to be on trees in recently built-up areas. Fading flowers have white petals and a dark red eye, and appear at a casual glance to be another species.

The **Black Cherry**, *Prunus serotina*, grows in North and South America, and may reach 35m tall in some areas of the eastern United States. It was introduced in 1629, but is not often seen here as a tree. More frequently it is found as bushes and seeds itself around in thickets on the edges of estates or on commons. This is because at one time it was planted as cover for pheasants and to provide them with a supply of the berry-like cherries. Many other birds eat them too and they spread widely on good light soils.

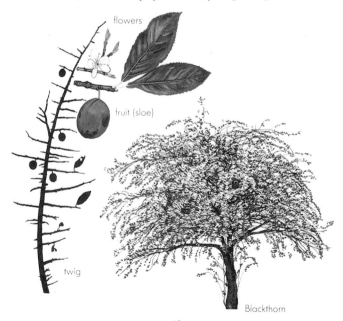

flowers

fruit (sloe)

twig

Blackthorn

Blackthorn, *Prunus spinosa*, is a spiny suckering shrub that grows wild all over the British Isles. It can be trained into a small tree but is most common in country hedges. The wild bushes are valued for their fruits, which are sloes, and long-tailed tits favour the plants as they make low, relatively dog-proof nesting places. Blackthorn is a great ornament to country hedges when in flower.

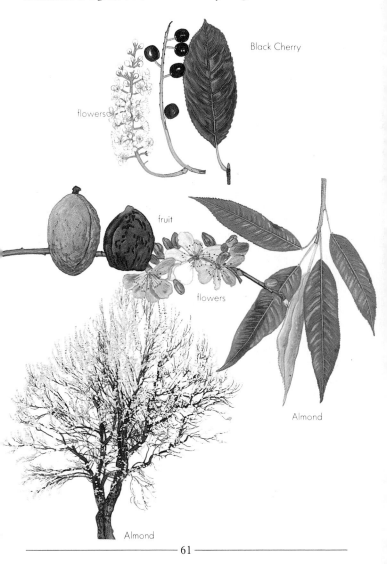

Black Cherry

flowers

fruit

flowers

Almond

Almond

Cherries & Plums

The **Wild Cherry** or Gean, *Prunus avium*, is a native tree of great value in decorative plantings. The young trees have a highly unusual form, with rising branches in well-spaced whorls on the trunk with bare lengths between them. The shoots are wreathed in sprays of single large white flowers as the leaves unfold, and the little berry-like cherries are eaten by birds as they turn red in August. The leaves turn yellow, orange and dark red in autumn.

The timber is very strong with a beautiful figure and takes a high polish, but is not durable out of doors. Trees are grown for the furniture trade in the Chilterns. The Gean has a powerful, spreading but superficial root system very ready to send up suckers. It is used as a rootstock for grafts of the Japanese cherries, but its suckers are a drawback.

The **Double Gean,** 'Plena', is magnificent in flower, with sprays of large, double flowers below bright green opening leaves.

The **Myrobalan Plum,** *Prunus cerasifera*, is not known wild but is common in England in semi-wild hedges and suburban gardens. It is a twiggy, bushy tree and the first to flower, covered in little white flowers in February or March and often mistaken for Blackthorn. Some years it has little red plums.

A common variety of it is **Pissard's Plum,** 'Pissardii', which now pervades suburbia like privet. It has a rather shapeless crown, with brownish-red or muddy purple leaves following the rather pretty, starry white flowers which open from pink buds. A much improved variety, 'Nigra', has shiny, dark red leaves and rich pink flowers which open a week later and last longer.

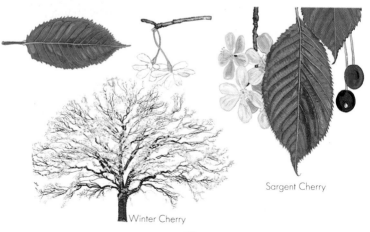

Sargent Cherry

Winter Cherry

The **Sargent Cherry**, *Prunus sargentii*, from Japan is very common in towns, with a spreading head of stout red-brown branches. Its fine pink clouds of blossom appear after the Almonds have faded. The dark, sharply toothed leaves hang lifelessly in summer but turn scarlet and deep red in early autumn.

The **Winter Cherry**, *Prunus subhirtella*, 'Autumnalis', opens its nearly white flowers among the yellowing leaves of autumn, and throughout the winter pinker and more double flowers appear, renewed after each sharp frost which kills them, until a final burst of flowers appears in April among the new leaves.

flowers

Double Gean

Myrobalan Plum

Wild Cherry

fruit

fruits

flowers

Pissard's Plum

Wild Cherry

Pissard's Plum

Japanese Cherries

The very floriferous, late-flowering, mostly double **Japanese Cherries** are selections from hybrids raised long ago in Japan. They are ornamental as opposed to eating cherries. Their precise origins are unknown but their copper red-brown young leaves derive from the Hill Cherry, *Prunus serrulata*. They all have big leaves tapering to a point and sharp, whisker-ended teeth. They begin to flower at the beginning of April and the sequence in which they come into flower is almost unchanging.

The first to flower is **'Shirotae'**, a flat, widely spreading, low tree with big white flowers in long-stemmed bunches below unfolding bright green leaves.

Next comes **'Taihaku'** with the biggest flowers of any cherry, often 7cm across, single, opening from a pink globular bud to pure white, beneath dark red unfolding leaves. It had been lost for 200 years in Japan, but a dying tree was found in a Sussex garden in 1923 and all the trees now in the world derive from this one.

'Ukon' opens its flowers primrose yellow beneath khaki brown leaves at about the same time. They fade to white as the leaves go green, then resemble those of 'Taihaku' with a similar red eye, but they are semi-double with more than five petals.

'Kanzan' has been the universal Japanese cherry for a long time now, planted by the million. It has an early strong growth and an abundance of flowers but the dark pink buds among dark brown unfolding leaves are not pretty.

'Shimidsu' opens its flowers with pink buds among unfolding leaves covered in violet hairs. The big flowers are snow-white and frilled, but the tree is a poor grower.

'Amanogawa' is the tightly erect cherry, opening rather untidily with age and at its best when a few years old and encrusted with

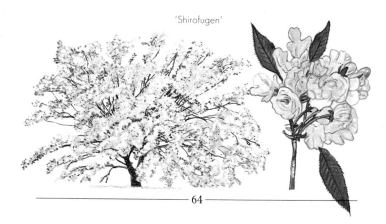

'Shirofugen'

large bunches of wide open, semi-double, pink and white, fragrant flowers.

'Shirofugen' is the last to flower and a fitting climax. Soft pink globular buds hang beneath rich dark red leaves, and then open to very big, double, frilled flowers, pink at first and then dazzling white. The leaves then turn green and the flowers turn pink again. This tree has a flat crown of level branches drooping at their tips.

'Shirotae'

'Taihaku'

'Kanzan'

Laburnums & others

The **Common Laburnum**, *Laburnum anagyroides*, was brought to Britain from its native southern Europe at least 400 years ago. It spreads by seeds, is short-lived and poisonous in all its parts. The yellow sapwood and brown heartwood polish well and are sought after for turnery and carving. The **Scotch Laburnum**, *Laburnum alpinum*, comes from the southern Alps but does grow particularly well in Scotland. It is a stronger growing, bigger-leafed tree than the Common Laburnum, and its smaller flowers are densely set, on longer heads.

The hybrid between these two, **Voss's Laburnum**, *Laburnum x watereri* 'Vossii', has long tassels densely set with big flowers.

The **Locust Tree**, *Robinia pseudoacacia*, is often called Acacia or simply 'Robinia'. It comes from the Allegheny Mountains and Mississippi Valley in the United States and was brought to England in 1638. It grows in sites too inhospitable for other trees, as with its roots in dry soil under pavings and its top in a windy corner, hot in summer and cold in winter. It will thrive on sterile mine spoil-heaps, able to grow there because of the nitrogen-fixing bacteria in nodules on its roots. It is good in cities and industrial areas partly because it has a short season in leaf in England, opening its leaves in June and discarding them in September. In more favourable conditions its vigour can be a nuisance for its root suckers can grow 2m of spined shoots in a year, far from the original tree. It does need warm summers and is not a good tree north of the Midlands.

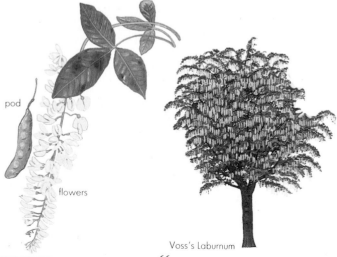

pod

flowers

Voss's Laburnum

Unless there is a good warm period in June it does not bear many flowers the following year and it needs another warm period in that year to open them properly. In cold weather the leaves remain half folded and the flowers scarcely open.

The **Golden Acacia**, 'Frisia', is a feature somewhere in almost every recent planting scheme in southern England. The oldest British trees date from about 1950 and are now 14m tall. Unexpectedly the foliage greened considerably in the hot summers of 1976 and 1983, while in normal cool summers it remains butter yellow until turning orange for autumn.

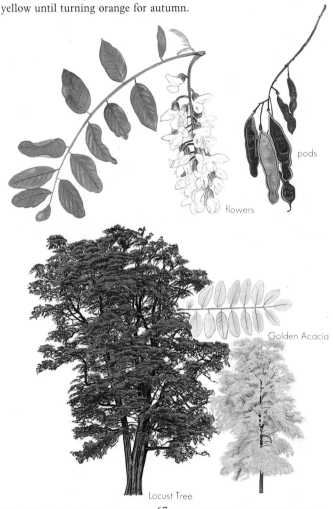

pods

flowers

Golden Acacia

Locust Tree

Tree of Heaven & others

The **Tree of Heaven**, *Ailanthus altissima*, is not really deserving of its name, since it rarely attains 26m in height. It was introduced from China in 1751 and thrives in the southern cities of England where it rapidly makes a fine, clean, pewter-grey bole marked by buff or silver streaks, but becomes prone to shed branches. The leaves unfold very late in the season, deep red, and only just fully out by the end of June. They fall early without colouring. They are normally about 50cm long with 15 leaflets. Each leaflet has one or more large, broad teeth or small lobes at the base, with a distinctive raised gland on it. The trees are either male or female, and in most years females bear many bunches of fruit, highly attractive when scarlet but very different when dismal brown in winter.

The **Honeylocust**, *Gleditsia triacanthos*, in its natural range grows in the Mississippi Basin in the United States, but it is now planted in most American cities. In Britain it feels the need of hot summers and thrives mainly in Cambridge, London and Chichester. Its autumn colour should be a good gold, but it is fleeting in Britain and its main merits in this country are its tolerance of hot dry places and its pretty leaves. It does not often bear fruits in Britain, an advantage since they can cause inconvenience when they fall, being large and solid. The ferocious, bunched spines on the trunk constitute its main disadvantage, but 'Inermis', the form planted in most cities, is without them.

The **Judas Tree**, *Cercis siliquastrum*, has flowers growing on the previous year's shoots, on branches and even on the bole. Following a hot summer, they are abundant in the next year, providing there is a hot May to bring them out. This species really only does well in southeast Britain. The tree is slow in growth and tends to be long-lived, although old trees tend to lie down.

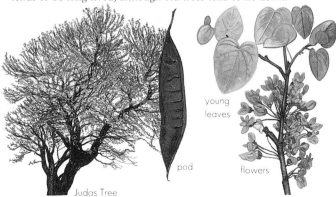

young
leaves

pod

flowers

Judas Tree

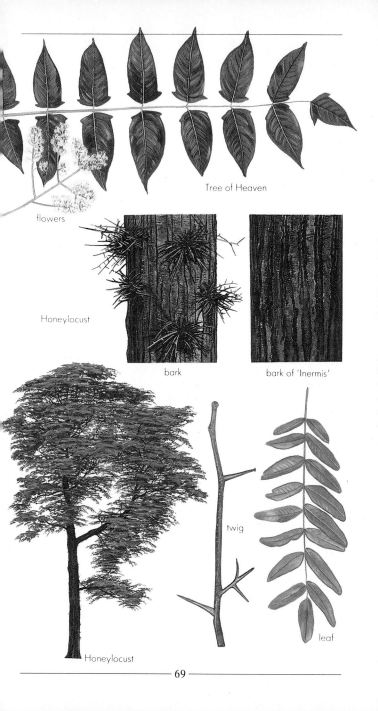

Tree of Heaven

flowers

Honeylocust

bark

bark of 'Inermis'

Honeylocust

twig

leaf

Holly & Box

The **Common Holly**, *Ilex aquifolium*, is a native tree growing on almost any soil, from chalk downs to mountain streamsides and deep woodland. It will grow in shade in oak and beech woods but will scarcely flower there, while in open hedgerows the trees are densely leafed, prolific in flower and conical with a spire top. The familiar crinkled spined leaves are replaced on old wood above the lower crown by elliptical leaves without teeth. The crinkled leaves distinguish this holly and some of its forms from the hybrid Highclere hollies. Every year female trees produce red berries, some of which are eaten by birds, while most remain on the trees until the following May.

Many forms of Common Holly are in cultivation. Laurel-leaf Holly, 'Laurifolia', has elliptical flat untoothed leaves and a narrow crown, up to 20m high. Hedgehog Holly, 'Ferox', has leaves with rows of short spines on the upper surface. 'Handsworth New Silver' has purple shoots and toothed leaves with white margins. 'Golden Milkmaid' has gold-splashed, toothed leaves and a similar male form is 'Golden Milkboy'.

The **Highclere Hollies**, *Ilex* x *altaclerensis*, arose at Highclere in Hampshire in 1838, but also arose at many other mansions at other times. They were formed when the tender Madeira Holly, *Ilex perado*, grown in tubs in conservatories in winter, were put out on the terraces in summer. Their flowers were pollinated by bees coming from Common Holly, and the plants raised from the seed were hybrid.

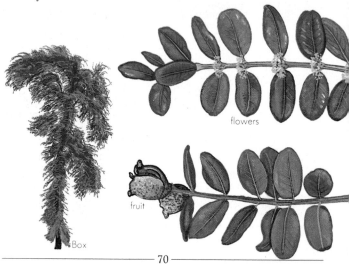

flowers

fruit

Box

Cultivars of Highclere Hollies include 'Hodginsii', a robust form which can grow in industrial cities and on sea fronts and 'Hendersonii', an equivalent female tree. 'Golden King' has solid, almost untoothed leaves with golden margins. 'Wilsonii' has the most handsome, polished, boldly toothed leaves of all.

The **Box**, *Buxus sempervirens*, is a native tree, growing on the North Downs, the Chilterns and in the Cotswolds. The best trees have shapely, narrowly conic crowns with dense hanging foliage and a clean bole; they grow up to 6m tall. In gardens, Box is more often a broad, not very densely branched bush. The flowers open in March and are unusual in their arrangements, there being six males around a central female. The wood is the heaviest of the native timbers and will not float in water.

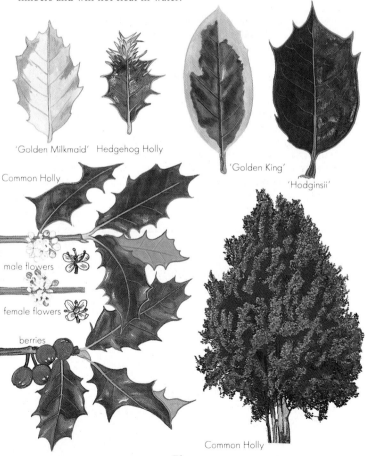

'Golden Milkmaid'   Hedgehog Holly

'Golden King'

'Hodginsii'

Common Holly

male flowers

female flowers

berries

Common Holly

Sycamore & other Maples

The **Sycamore**, *Acer pseudoplatanus*, is easily the biggest of the European maples; it ranges widely across the middle of Europe and was brought to Britain at least 400 years ago. It spreads rapidly by seed in woods and cities, where it is as impervious to pollution as it is to salt-laden winds on the coast. In woods it is liable to take over, its leathery leaves make mats which suppress the flowers and grasses and birds dislike it. It is a very long-lived tree and many grow to huge size. The wood is ideal for kitchenware as it is white, hard and can be scrubbed without the grain picking up, takes no stain from nor taints the food. It also polishes well and can be cut to give the pretty grain used in string instruments.

Among its many cultivars are 'Variegatum', an old variety often seen in parks and gardens; 'Leopoldii' with cream-splashed leaves; and 'Brilliantissimum' with leaves that turn from red to pink, orange, white and green as they age.

The **Norway Maple**, *Acer platanoides*, ranges widely across Europe and was probably brought to Britain after 1600. It is vigorous and healthy, and widely used in amenity plantings. Its flowers have big petals for a maple and shine out a brilliant acid-yellow in March or April. It has a leafy crown with butter yellow leaves in autumn.

There are many cultivars of Norway Maple, including 'Crimson King' with rich ruby red leaves; 'Goldsworth Purple', with duller red leaves which is often mistaken for 'Crimson King'; and Drummond's Maple, 'Drummondii' with variegated leaves, often seen in suburban areas.

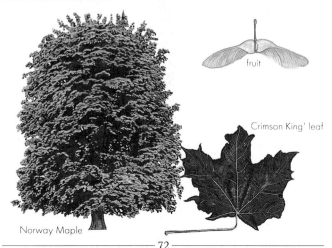

fruit

Crimson King' leaf

Norway Maple

The **Italian Maple**, *Acer opalus*, looks like Sycamore in summer and winter, but in spring it has soft yellow, hanging flowers with large petals and in autumn its leaves turn rich orange, yellow and brown. It comes from Italy, grows well in Britain but is not often planted except in the London parks.

fruit

flowers

Italian Maple

Sycamore

fruits

twig

Sycamore

Field Maple & others

The **Field Maple**, *Acer campestre*, is the only maple native to Britain. It is a tree of chalk and limestone soils and is most common in and near the chalklands of southern England. It is often seen in a clipped hedge but when it grows into a hedgerow tree with plenty of room it has a large domed crown of curved branches and straight shoots, to 15m or more tall, and a stout bole often much encumbered by burrs and sprouts. Autumn colours vary from dark red and purple to old gold and russet, depending on where the tree is growing. It is a tough tree, able to grow in city parks but rather dark and dull.

The **Ashleaf Maple**, *Acer negundo*, is commonly planted in town gardens, usually in its form 'Variegatum', a female tree with boldly white-variegated, ash-like leaves. Even the wings of the fruits are white, stained pale purple or pink. The tree, in its original green form, is native to North America but this tree has dull foliage in Britain and is rarely seen.

The **Smooth Japanese Maple**, *Acer palmatum*, was brought to Britain from Japan in 1820. Often seen as a front garden shrub, it grows in woodland gardens to over 15m tall. The leaves may turn yellow, orange or red in autumn. It is often grown in the form

leaf of 'Atropurpureum'

leaf

Japanese Maple 'Vitifolium'

leaf of 'Osakazuki'

Smooth Japanese Maple

'Atropurpureum' with red leaves; but the best form is 'Osakazuki' with large, seven-lobed leaves, green in summer when the bunches of scarlet fruit hang beneath them, and flame scarlet in October. Unlike other trees turning red in autumn, this one does not need a fully sunlit position to do so and so is valuable for a shady site.

The **Downy Japanese Maple**, *Acer japonicum*, grows into a small tree with many sinuous, upright, smooth grey stems and purple flowers in nodding bunches, seen before the leaves unfold fully. 'Vitifolium' is a bigger tree, up to 14m tall, with bigger leaves and dazzling autumn colours, in bright royal-red, gold, orange and green.

Variegated Ashleaf Maple

Field Maple

flowers

Ashleaf Maple

fruit

Field Maple

Horse Chestnut

The **Horse Chestnut**, *Aesculus hippocastanum*, masquerades very successfully as a native British tree without which no village green nor rectory lawn is complete, although it was unknown even to botanists until 1596. It was introduced between 1605 and 1617 and is native only to a few mountains in Greece and Albania. It really does not look like a native of Britain when laden with panicles of showy flowers.

The wood is amongst the best for toys and artificial limbs because it is light, works easily and does not splinter. On the other hand its weakness can make the tree dangerous, when a sudden shower of rain may be enough to break out a heavy limb as the leaves become sodden. These trees rarely have long lives, and trees about 150 years old may decay and collapse, especially when they have been cut back.

There is great variation in the time when the leaves and flowerheads expand. Many areas have one tree that is almost in leaf and bud in early March, while other trees are still in bud until the end of April and their flowers open in May.

Horse Chestnuts can be a source of danger in conker time from the fall out of assorted missiles. An alternative is to plant the sterile, double-flowered 'Baumanii' although some consider this unsporting and an omission of an essential autumn feature of the tree. The flowers of 'Baumanii' are frilly and pretty but not, from a distance, any more showy than those of the single form. They fade to a brown mush of petals.

The **Red Horse Chestnut**, *Aesculus* x *carnea*, probably arose in Germany as a hybrid between the Common Horse Chestnut and the American Red Buckeye, *Aesculus pavia*, and was being

Red Horse Chestnut

flower

fruit

bark

twig

marketed by 1820. By a quirk of genetics, it is not only fertile but breeds true despite its hybrid origin. By the time the tree is 17m tall it is disfigured by big craters of canker, crumbling inside and will not survive for long.

Horse Chestnut

flowers

twig

fruit

Horse Chestnut

Limes

The **Broadleaf Lime**, *Tilia platyphyllos*, is native to some woods on old limestone from the Wye Gorge to the Pennines, but it is very local in the wild. It is widely but not abundantly planted in parks, and here and there in streets or in avenues it replaces the Common Lime. The bowl-shaped crown of young trees later becomes less regular but they still remain finely domed and free of excrescences, in stark contrast to the Common Lime as usually seen. Neither the stem nor the base sprouts suckers. The flowers are the first of all the limes to open and are fragrant like those of Common Lime. The fruits remain on the lower branches after the leaves have been shed, a useful way to identify the tree.

The **Small-leaf Lime**, *Tilia cordata*, is the other native British lime, and is locally an important feature of some woods from Avon to Cumbria. Before Saxon times it was more prominent than Oak, but its seedlings are readily grazed and it was so useful that it was extinguished very early in most forests. It is long-lived and spreads by suckers; one such circle in Westonbirt is judged to be over 1000 years old. It is widely planted, beside roadsides and in gardens and is most easily recognised when its flowers shine out as yellow stars at all angles, very different from the flowers of other limes which hang below big bracts.

The **Common Lime**, *Tilia* x *europaea*, is presumed to be a hybrid between the Broadleaf and Small-leaf Limes but its early history is unknown. It is one of the most abundant, widespread and

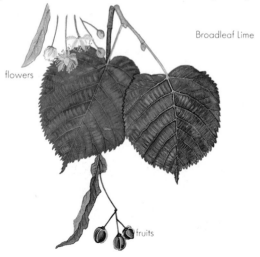

flowers

Broadleaf Lime

fruits

large trees, planted in streets and avenues. As a tree for town streets, the Common Lime has no rival for bottom place. It has roots good at lifting paving; it casts dense shade; it fails to colour in autumn; and is hugely infested with greenfly which rain sticky honeydew on its leaves and on anything in its shade. In addition the trees sprout so vigorously from the base that they need cutting back annually, and they also become very tall, up to 42m in height.

under

flws

flowers

Small-leaf Lime

fruits

flowers

Common Lime

Common Lime

fruits

Eucalyptus Trees

The Myrtle family is a huge one, with evergreen, aromatic plants bearing flowers with prominent bunches of stamens. They are found throughout the warmer regions of the world. The Eucalypts or Gums are in several ways the most remarkable trees in the world. They dominate the land mass of Australia; they include the tallest known broadleaf trees, not only in their native woods, but also, less than 100 years after they were planted, in most other countries in warm regions; they hold all the records for growth in their first few years, up to 60m tall; they set no winter buds at all, but merely pause in their growth until any cold period passes; and lastly, in juvenile growth they have opposite, rounded leaves, clasping the stem or combined into a circle around the stem, but soon turn to bearing adult alternate, long, slender leaves.

The **Blue Gum**, *Eucalyptus globulus*, is largely confined to Tasmania as a native tree and is not there one of the tallest gums, but it has rapidly overtaken all other broadleafed trees almost everywhere it has been planted. In Britain, this is true in Ireland and the Isle of Man, but in mainland Britain it has never survived long enough to make any impact. The trees stand up to 35m tall in almost every other garden on the coast south of Dublin, whereas in Wales, which is visible across the sea on a clear day, they cannot survive many winters.

The **Cider Gum**, *Eucalyptus gunnii*, is the standard garden Eucalypt, and has run wild in Brightlingsea on the Essex coast.

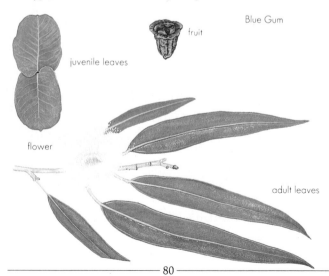

Blue Gum

fruit

juvenile leaves

flower

adult leaves

Normally completely hardy it was killed here and there, in the winters of 1979 and 1981, but survives to be common in gardens everywhere. It was introduced in 1845 from Tasmania, where it is native, and the tallest trees in Britain are now over 30m high. The flowers are borne prolifically after ten years and open from June until the autumn.

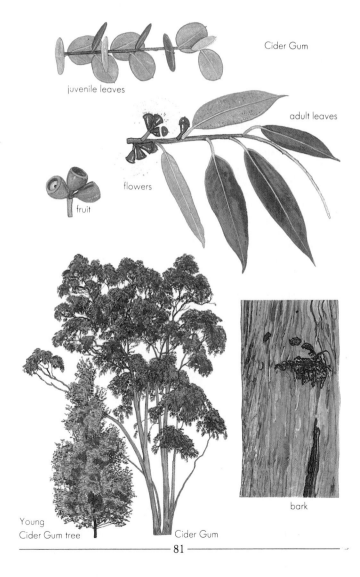

Cider Gum

juvenile leaves

adult leaves

flowers

fruit

Young Cider Gum tree

Cider Gum

bark

Ash Trees

The **Common Ash**, *Fraxinus excelsior*, is native to the British Isles and grows to the furthest north, preferring limestone soils. It leafs out late and has an open light crown but is often overgrown with ivy. Ashes have been known to attain heights of 45m, but only in sheltered valleys and they seldom live more than 200 years. The flowers of Common Ash lack petals and sometimes a tree may be all male or all female. Often only a few branches on a tree will bear fruits. The fruits form an important food for bullfinches, and a good season for ash fruits may lessen damage to fruit trees.

The **Manna Ash**, *Fraxinus ornus*, is one of the select group of ashes that has petals on the flowers and a strong scent. All but one come from Asia, but the Manna Ash spreads into southern Europe. Despite its southern origin the tree grows well in Britain, into southern Scotland. It grows at a moderate rate and is planted along some arterial roads in London. Although it grows from fresh seeds, most planted trees are grafted onto Common Ash and can be identified in winter, by the change at grafting level from criss-crossed ridged bark to smooth dull grey, and by the broadly domed crown and brown buds. The bright shiny green flowers open white in June; their scent is sweetish and reminiscent of dusty upholstery.

The **Narrowleaf Ash**, *Fraxinus angustifolia*, is a species from the African and European shores of the western Mediterranean. It should therefore be accustomed to hot dry summers and wet winters and is common only in London. There are very few trees north of the Thames. Nearly all the big trees have been grafted on to the Common Ash and the union is often grossly swollen, with the Narrowleaf making more growth than the rootstock and the

Narrowleaf Ash

female flowers

bark changing just below the swelling from shallowly ridged, pale grey Common Ash bark to very rough, knobbly, almost black Narrowleaf bark. The bright smooth foliage is light and attractive against this dark bark, particularly in the variety *lentiscifolia* in which the leaves hang and have more widely spaced leaflets. About a third of the trees are of this variety.

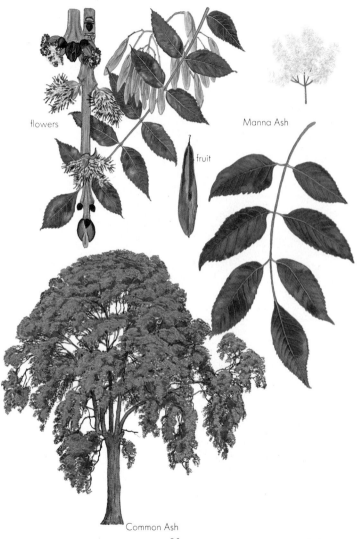

flowers

fruit

Manna Ash

Common Ash

Strawberry Tree

The **Strawberry Tree**, *Arbutus unedo*, is native to the British Isles, but only to southern Ireland where it forms low dense scrub on some exposed cliff tops. In England it needs shelter and is most often found in church yards and village gardens. It is very slow-growing, rarely exceeding 11m in height, and not long-lived, usually no more than a tall bush with branches arising from a bole bent parallel to the ground.

The tree is at its best in October and November when the flowers are out and last year's fruit turn from green to scarlet via yellow. It has dull grey, fissured bark like an oak and dark red branches. The wood is very dense and fine-grained, pale pink and dark brown in colour but splits and twists very badly when drying.

fruits

Strawberry Tree

Catalpa

The **Catalpa**, *Catalpa bignonioides*, is also called the Indian Bean-tree, a misleading name as the Indians concerned were Red Indians and the fruits are neither pods nor do they hold beans. It is native to a narrow belt of the United States from Louisiana to Florida, but is now grown all over the States and was brought to Britain in 1726. It needs hot summers to grow and flower well, and is a good flowering tree valuable for its late season in August, within the region south and east of a line from Bath to Cambridge, particularly in London.

Golden Catalpa, 'Aurea', is more tender than the type tree and can also scorch in direct sunlight, so is not an easy tree to grow well and is only seen north as far as Leamington Spa.

leaf

flowers

Golden Catalpa   Catalpa

Palms

The **Cabbage Tree**, *Cordyline australis*, is not a true palm but an agave, related to the Yuccas. It is native to New Zealand and was first sent to Britain in 1823. It thrives near the west coast, even to the extreme north of Scotland, in the Isle of Man and Ireland. This tree can branch only where it bears a flower; it has very strong leaves and thick, corky bark.

True Palms may have leaves like fans or pinnate leaves like feathers. The only palm hardy outside Torquay and the Isles of Scilly is the **Chusan Palm**, *Trachycarpus fortunei*, brought from south China in 1839. It is quite a hardy tree and can be grown in the Midlands north to Lancashire and into Scotland on the west coast. Growth is very slow, a tree planted in 1843 at Kew is only 10m tall, and the mode of growth gives only minimal increase in diameter, so the stem remains slender. It looks much stouter than it is when the big leaf bases adhere to the trunk with a thick cover of fibres. This palm flowers freely almost everywhere, with several huge flower heads each summer.

The **Canary Palm**, *Phoenix canariensis*, is a pinnate-leafed palm, and the noblest of the tribe, with a crown of a hundred or more leaves up to 6m long. In Britain it grows only in the Isles of Scilly,

Canary Palm

Dwarf Fan-palm

Canary Palm leaf

County Cork and the Channel Islands. However, this palm is common in warmer countries.

The **Dwarf Fan-palm**, *Chamaerops humilis*, is the only palm wild in Europe where it covers hillsides in Sicily, Spain and the south of France, but it is no more than a hard, spiny shrub, occasionally 1.5m tall in Britain.

fruit

Cabbage Tree leaf

Chusan Palm

fruits

leaf

'trunk'

Cabbage Tree

Chusan Palm

CONIFERS

Maidenhair Tree

The **Maidenhair Tree**, *Ginkgo biloba*, is the last survivor of an entire Order of plants that dominated the forests of the world 150 million years ago. It is a ginkgo, neither a broadleaf tree nor a conifer. Its leaves are unlike any other, with a broad close fan of radiating veins. They are shed in winter, turning gold and then orange in warm autumns, before falling. Male and female flowers grow on separate trees; male trees seldom flower until 150 years old but female trees may flower when less than 50 years old and then produce many fruits. Most trees in Britain have yet to flower.

The present species survived only in China. It was brought to Europe in around 1730. The tree planted then, in Utrecht, is still there. In China, trees live to an immense age and they should also do so in Europe, since none of their insect pests survive here and only Honey Fungus is sometimes fatal. They need summer warmth, so size declines markedly towards the north.

male catkins emerging

fruit

female flowers

leaf

Maidenhair Tree

Monkey-puzzle Tree

The **Chile Pine**, *Araucaria araucana*, was given the nickname 'Monkey-puzzler' by the Victorians after a visitor to Cornwall was shown one of the first to arrive in this country, and exclaimed 'Well, it would puzzle a monkey to climb that!' It grows as a native tree on the Chile-Argentina border.

It has whorled branches on a stout, nearly cylindrical bole and large, leathery leaves. The cones are large, globular and spiny and grow on separate trees from the thick, drooping male catkins. The cones hold over a hundred seeds and should be over 95% fertile if a male is nearby. Old trees often throw up sprouts from around the base, or where surface roots have been damaged, a good distance away. This is usually the true origin of many taken to be self-sown seedlings.

cone

shoot

Monkey-puzzle

Yews

The Yews are a group of conifers, much more primitive than those which bear cones. Each berry-like fruit has a single large seed, partially enclosed in a succulent red aril which grows up around it. The seed is, like the foliage, very poisonous to people and many animals, but deer and rabbits eat the leaves without harm. Yew has extremely strong and durable wood, a factor which enables old trees to hold together and support long branches, even when a relatively thin ring of live wood around the hollow bole is all that is left.

The **Common Yew**, *Taxus baccata*, is nearly immortal, resistant to almost every pest and disease of importance, and immune to stress from exposure, drought and cold. It is by a long way the longest living tree we have and many in country churchyards are certainly much older than the churches, often thousands of years old. Since the yews predate the churches, the sites may have been holy sites and the yews sacred trees, possibly symbols of immortality, under which the Elders met.

The biggest yews are almost all in churchyards, often on sheltered, locally raised ground above a stream, where they are not subject to flooding (yews can tolerate anything else). The church was placed so that the yews gave shelter from the snow and cold winds to parishioners in places where they might need to wait – the lych gate, the porch and the path between. No tradition is known of planting a yew when a church is built.

The **Irish Yew**, 'Fastigiata' was found as two nearby plants in Ireland in about 1770 by a farmer, and no other has ever been

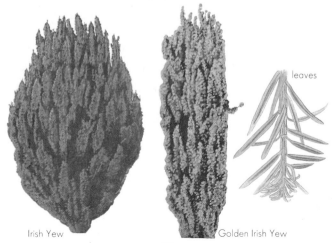

leaves

Irish Yew   Golden Irish Yew

found. All the modern trees come from one of these. They are female, with the leaves in whorls around vertical shoots. Avenues of Irish Yews are frequently seen in western gardens but are very gloomy. Many trees are bent out of shape by snow, but when clipped carefully they can be a fine feature. The Golden Irish Yew, 'Fastigiata Aurea', is a similar golden form.

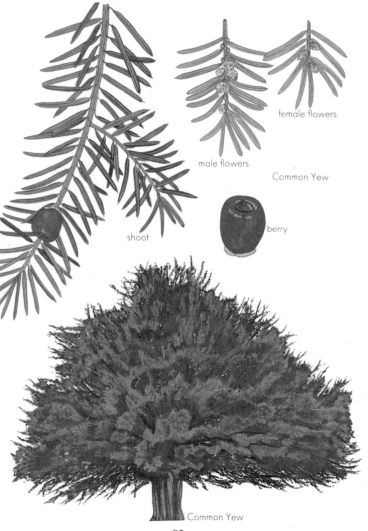

female flowers

male flowers

Common Yew

shoot

berry

Common Yew

Cypresses

The **Leyland Cypress**, *Cupressocyparis leylandii*, arose in 1888 in Wales when seeds were raised from a Nootka Cypress; all six plants raised still stand today at Haggerston Castle. It arose again in 1911 in the same garden when seed was picked from a Monterey Cypress.

The hybrid vigour of the plant shows in its fast growth, in its indifference to soil, polluted air and, to some extent, exposure and sea winds. It is extensively planted in towns and suburbs. 'Haggerston Grey' is the commonest form, and has slender, well-separated, fine shoots often showing some grey. 'Leighton Green' is less common but is most likely to be found in older gardens. It has long, ferny, very green, flattened sprays. It flowers freely while 'Haggerston Grey' rarely flowers at all. 'Castlewellan Gold' will diversify the impending urban forests as it grows about as fast and is being planted with abandon.

The **Lawson Cypress**, *Chamaecyparis lawsoniana*, is, in its various forms, the dominant tree of British gardens, parks and suburbs. It brings shape, shelter, background and diversity of colour and form to garden design; without it urban bird-life would be much poorer. It comes from western North America where it is a dark sea-green and narrowly conical tree to 60m tall. It is inexplicable that so uniform a forest tree should, from its earliest years in cultivation in Europe, become the most prolific source of variants in colour, form and foliage of all the world's conifers.

'Erecta viridis' was the first variant to arise, in Surrey in 1855. A much improved form of this variant, 'Green Spire' appeared in

'Stewartii' 'Fletcheri' 'Columnaris' 'Alumii' 'Lutea'

1945. 'Allumii' is the commonest conifer seen in small gardens or backing onto roads; 'Pottenii' is good for formal planting in a line or group; 'Columnaris' has been widely planted since it arose in 1950. The fluffy, dark blue-grey foliage of 'Fletcheri' is familiar everywhere, as is a seedling which came from it, 'Ellwoodii', with more adult, greyer foliage. The slender 'Lutea' was the earliest good golden form, and 'Stewartii', with a very different, broadly conical form, is becoming just as familiar.

Lawson Cypress

'Haggerston Grey'

cone

'Leighton Green'

Lawson Cypress

Leyland Cypress

Junipers

The **Common Juniper**, *Juniperus communis*, has the most extensive range worldwide, of any tree. It is the only one growing in the wild on both sides of the Atlantic Ocean, one of the very few to cross North America to the Pacific Ocean, and to span Europe and Siberia to reach that ocean on its opposite side. Its distribution in Britain is eccentric. On chalk and limestone in England it grows in fully open, sunny places; but on wet acid peat in the north of Scotland, where the sunshine is much less strong, it grows in the shady woods of old Scots Pines. It grows very slowly in the wild and few trees exceed 5m. The **Dwarf Juniper**, var. *nana*, grows at high altitudes in northern Britain and in Irish bogs; it has softer, less prickly foliage.

Common Juniper is very rare in gardens but the **Irish Juniper** 'Hibernica' is quite common. It is often planted to give a vertical contrast to low hummock plants in rock gardens or amongst heaths, and grows 7–9m tall. The **Swedish Juniper**, 'Suecica' is less tall and has nodding tips to its shoots; it is less frequent.

The **Chinese Juniper**, *Juniperus chinensis*, is by far the commonest tree-juniper in gardens and parks, although distinctly uncommon in Scotland. It has a deeply fluted bole, sometimes more

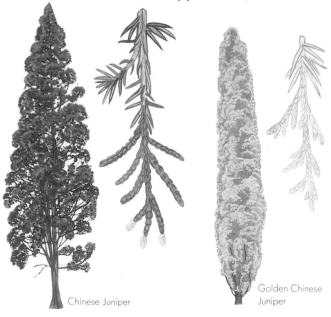

Chinese Juniper

Golden Chinese Juniper

like two stems roughly fused together. The juvenile foliage is spiny and hard, so it is better to crush the adult smooth shoots to find the slightly sour resinous scent. The Golden Chinese Juniper 'Aurea' is common in towns in southern England but less widely seen in the north. It is a male tree, with many shoots entirely clad in juvenile foliage and with many yellow flowers for much of the year.

Meyer's Blue Juniper, *Juniperus squamata* 'Meyeri', is a garden selection of a widespread and variable Himalayan and Chinese juniper. It is now amongst the most commonly planted junipers in small-scale features, a perhaps unwise place for it, since it soon spreads widely in an irregular table-top manner with many acute peaks. It begins life as such a neat little conical, dense, electric blue cutting that its later development is not often foreseen.

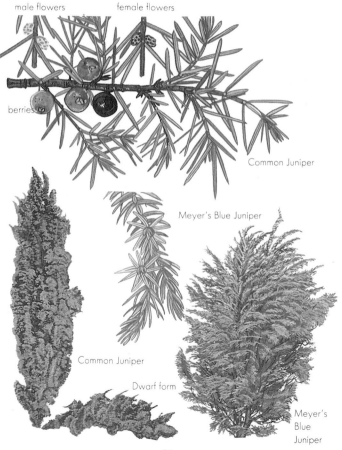

male flowers

female flowers

berries

Common Juniper

Meyer's Blue Juniper

Common Juniper

Dwarf form

Meyer's Blue Juniper

Red Cedars

The **Western Red Cedar**, *Thuja plicata*, was one of many cypresses and junipers called 'cedars' by settlers in North America. It comes from the Pacific coast area and was introduced into Britain in 1854. It was planted in almost every large garden as soon as it was available and throve in the cool damp north and west and on moist clay soils in the east. It has been planted as a crop on a local scale and yields a quick return of strong but light timber for ladders and goalposts. It is also valued for underplanting old oak, larch or beech where few other conifers would succeed, and is useful in shelterbelts to give them solidity.

The heavy, fruity scent of the foliage carries far from a group of trees in humid weather. Male flowers are minute and many cones are produced so that seedlings arise in large numbers around trees on damp soils. The form known as **Golden-barred Thuja**, 'Zebrina' is often planted in gardens. It varies in the amount and brightness of the gold in its foliage.

The **Northern White Cedar**, *Thuja occidentalis*, was probably the first American tree to be brought to Britain, either in 1536 or 1596. It rarely looks happy here, grows slowly, and gives up early. The foliage is slightly roughened above by a raised gland on each scale leaf and is uniformly matt pale green beneath. It has an array of cultivars. 'Lutea' is a robust, bright and healthy-looking tree with solid handsome foliage; 'Spiralis' sometimes shows some winter bronzing, a feature shown by other forms of the species.

The **Japanese Thuja**, *Thuja standishii*, has the most deliciously scented foliage of any conifer, sweet, lemony and spicy, and with a good hint of eucalyptus. The sprays of foliage are thick and heavy, often dusty blue-grey when new, and they nod at the branch tips. It is found in important gardens everywhere, sometimes 20m tall.

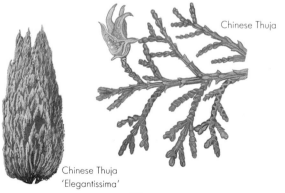

Chinese Thuja

Chinese Thuja
'Elegantissima'

The **Chinese Thuja**, *Thuja orientalis*, was introduced to Britain in 1752 and seems to be most common in village gardens in the Midlands. 'Elegantissima' is a semi-dwarf form much planted in tubs on patios, in rock gardens and around houses.

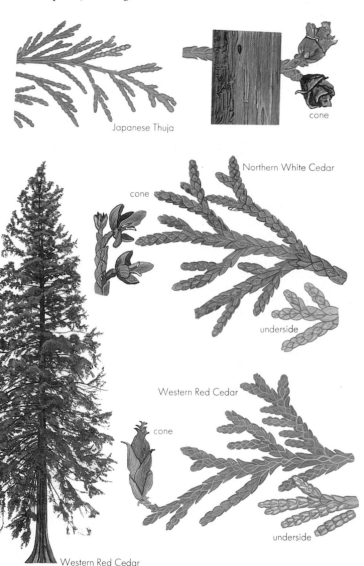

Japanese Thuja

cone

Northern White Cedar

cone

underside

Western Red Cedar

cone

underside

Western Red Cedar

Sequoias

The two Sequoias, the Giant Sequoia and the Coast Redwood, grow only in California and Oregon, in the United States.

The **Giant Sequoia**, *Sequoiadendron giganteum*, is well known to be the biggest tree in the world, not in height, nor in diameter, but in the two combined and therefore in volume of timber. The holder of this record is 'General Sherman' in Sequoia National Park, 83m tall and 24m in girth, measured 2m above ground level. The species was introduced to Britain in 1853 and was at once planted on every estate of any standing throughout the British Isles. Within 80 years or so, it was the biggest tree in every county, the lightning conductor of England, and, with its fibrous spongy bark the roosting place for tree creepers, as well as the tree that every schoolboy could punch with impunity. This tree has never blown down and many of those in Scotland, untroubled by lightning, could begin to rival those in California for height and diameter of bole. Seeds are produced but are not always viable, for once the male flowers begin to open they are vulnerable to frost, and are often caught.

The **Coast Redwood**, *Sequoia sempervirens*, grows a little inland from the Pacific coast of California and Oregon in its native haunts. The official tallest tree in the world is a Coast Redwood, 112m tall. This species came to Britain in 1843 and huge specimens grow in the west and north. The tree needs humid summers for it to grow rapidly for long and it needs at all times to be in deep shelter. It is scorched by freezing dry east winds but does grow, though more slowly, in towns and in eastern counties, where it tends to become thin in the crown.

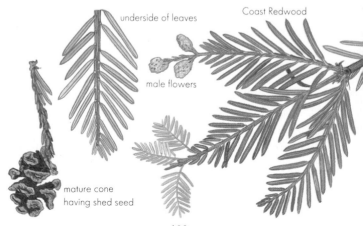

underside of leaves

Coast Redwood

male flowers

mature cone
having shed seed

male flowers

young cones

mature cone

bark

Giant Sequoia

Deciduous Redwoods

The **Swamp Cypress**, *Taxodium distichum*, was the first of the scattered and highly various remnant species of the Redwood family to become known to botanists. It was brought to England in about 1638, but its first planting in any numbers was probably in 1750, in Syon Park, where there are still a dozen or more.

This tree is thought to live for 1000 years or more in its native swamps in the eastern United States, and a dead or dying one in Britain is probably unknown. In all its range it enjoys long hot summers and this is reflected in Britain in that the big trees are all in the south. It is unusual amongst conifers in that it is deciduous and is late into leaf in Britain, only hazed with green in June and not fully leafed until July. It colours late in autumn and some trees may still hold foliage until December. Male catkins are prominent through the winter on many trees. Female flowers are borne on the same tree.

If the trees are growing on flooded ground, they produce 'knees' like wooden anthills, after they have been growing for about 45 years. They presumably help the tree to take air to the roots since they have very spongy woody tissues inside. The timber of the tree is very durable when repeatedly wetted and dried and has been imported for holding the glass in quality greenhouses.

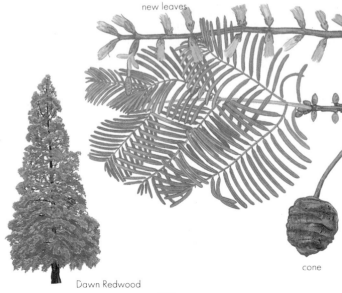

new leaves

cone

Dawn Redwood

The **Dawn Redwood**, *Metasequoia glyptostroboides*, had been a well-known fossil from rocks 80 – 100 million years old, all over the world. Then in 1945 details were published of trees that had been found growing around a paddyfield in China. The trees grow best beside water or in a damp hollow, in Britain. The Dawn Redwood differs from the Swamp Cypress in the leaves and shoots being opposite, the crown more open and the leaves bigger, broader and unfolding some two months earlier. Cones are numerous after a hot summer but no British summer has been hot enough to induce male flowers so the seeds are infertile.

Swamp Cypress

male catkins

cone

'knees' Swamp Cypress

Silver Firs

Silver Firs, *Abies* species, have smooth, leathery foliage whereas the leaves of spruces are hard and spined. Silver Firs hold their cones vertically until they break up on the tree, whereas spruce cones are hanging and shed complete.

The **European Silver Fir**, *Abies alba*, is the largest tree species in stature outside the Rocky Mountains. There are some magnificent natural stands on the northern slopes of the Pyrenees where they grow pure, and in eastern France where they grow among beech. The tree was planted extensively in Britain after 1700, but has now largely been replaced by American species. Young trees grow more sideways than upwards, until they are about four years old, when the leaders begin to dominate. When growing in the open, old trees tend to have many large branches which turn sharply upward near the bole. Every year these trees carry dense rows of the slender, pale green cones, but they are seen closely only when squirrels or high winds deposit some of the shoots on the ground.

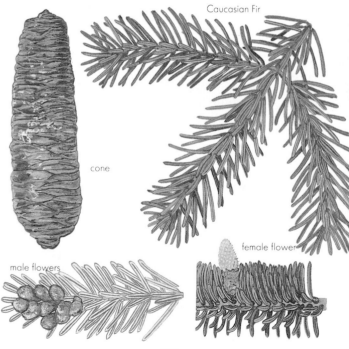

Caucasian Fir

cone

male flowers

female flower

The **Caucasian Fir**, *Abies nordmanniana*, is one of the commonest silver firs in gardens. However it does not do well near towns, and in many old gardens or estates encroached by buildings or industry there are specimens in poor condition. It is at its best in the cool glens of Scotland, Ireland or north Wales, the best trees having splendidly luxuriant foliage with bright shiny, long leaves crowded above the shoots. Cones are borne only on trees about 30m tall, not every year and only around the tip.

European Silver Fir

underside of leaves

female flower

cone

male flowers

European Silver Fir

Silver Firs

The **Grand Fir**, *Abies grandis*, comes from the Pacific coast areas of North America, where it grows over 80m tall in sheltered valleys. It was introduced to Britain in 1832 and grows very rapidly in shelter in cool, moist western and northern areas. Trees frequently exceed 50m in height. However it is sensitive to impure air and will barely grow near towns. It is common as a big specimen in the policy woods of Scottish castles and in small plantations in forests.

The smooth, leathery foliage of this tree has a strong scent of oranges when crushed. Few trees produce cones before they are 50 years old, the cones are sparsely borne and grow on top shoots 40m from the ground, so are little seen.

The **Noble Fir**, *Abies procera*, comes from Washington and Oregon in the United States and was sent to Britain in 1830. It is most at home in the eastern Scottish Highlands, from Aberdeen northwards, and seedlings spring up in great numbers there, in lines along rotting logs where they are present. Unless in a position sheltered from autumn gales, big trees are very likely to have broken tops with deformed thick, twisting branches. The tree is particularly susceptible to a mis-shapen top because it often bears numerous, big, heavy cones which bend the shoots, until the seeds are shed and the cones disintegrate in November.

Some of the trees belong to the variety, *glauca*, with very blue-white young foliage. This variety may be found in the wild, but specimens in gardens may be grafts from a particularly well-coloured tree.

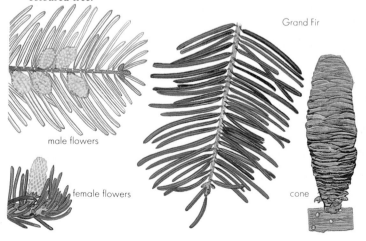

male flowers

female flowers

Grand Fir

cone

The **Korean Fir**, *Abies koreana*, is mostly seen as a semi-dwarf form which can be grown in shrubberies. It produces pink flowers and fine blue-purple cones when very young. It comes from an island off South Korea. The mainland form makes a shapely tree of moderate size.

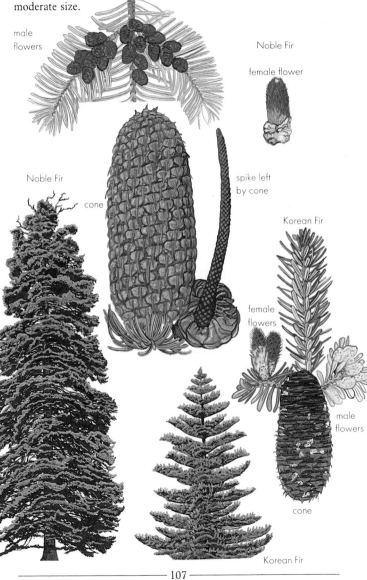

male flowers

Noble Fir

female flower

Noble Fir

cone

spike left by cone

Korean Fir

female flowers

male flowers

cone

Korean Fir

Douglas Fir

The **Douglas Fir**, *Pseudotsuga menziesii*, is one of the great trees of the world and may have been the tallest ever to grow. One was felled in 1895 on Vancouver Island that was 128m tall. Today a stand of trees in Washington State, in the western United States, has trees 85 – 90m tall. Seed was sent to Britain in 1827 and original trees from that packet are still numerous in this island, particularly in Scotland.

The trees grow well in Britain, the tallest reaching over 60m at the present time, with diameters around 150 – 190cm. Since the timber is strong and hard, such growth makes the tree of interest to foresters but its popularity waxes and wanes. It needs a deep, well-drained mineral soil and some shelter. It also suffers an apparent decline when about 20 years old after good growth, but normally regains its health after thinning. However, on some soils in some areas, like the Coal Measures, in south Wales, it is no longer planted since it does not do well.

Young plantations of Douglas Firs become very dark inside until thinning, shading out all vegetation beneath. In this stage, which is prolonged if thinning is neglected, these woods gave commercial forestry a bad name for impoverishing the countryside, but numbers of goldcrests breed there and, as more light is let in, more ground plants return. There is no point in letting Douglas Firs grow more than 40m tall, as the logs are then too big for ordinary equipment. However, in many forests, a ride-side line or belt, where the biggest trees grow, is left for its scenic value.

seed

cone variations

Douglas Fir

female flowers

male flowers

buds

Douglas Fir

Young tree

Cedars

The true Cedars are a group of four species from the
Mediterranean and western Himalayan regions.

The **Cedar of Lebanon**, *Cedrus libani*, grows in a small grove
on Mount Lebanon, Syria, and on the Taurus and Anti-taurus
Mountains in Turkey. It has been grown in Europe since 1638
when seed was brought to England and can be seen in many of the
big 'Capability Brown' gardens. It is a big spreading tree, up to
35m or more tall, and has one or several trunks and branches which
spread far and level, with the tips level or slightly drooping in old
trees. The length of the needles, useful in separating cedars, is
around 2.5cm.

The **Atlas Cedar**, *Cedrus atlantica* from the Atlas Mountains in
Algeria and Morocco, is almost always seen, planted in gardens and
churchyards, as one of the very grey-blue forms of the Blue Atlas
Cedar, var. *glauca*. The leaves are shorter than those of the Cedar
of Lebanon, the bark much paler gray and the branches arise at an
angle of about 45° with their tips at the same angle.

The **Deodar Cedar**, *Cedrus deodara*, has been reported to grow
70m tall in the Punjab, in the middle of its range from Afghanistan
along the Western Himalayas. It grows with a dropper leader,

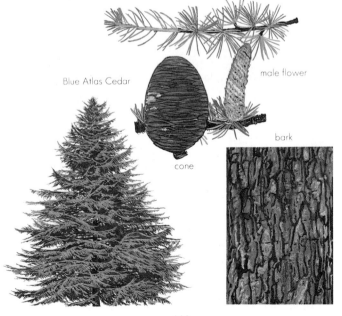

Blue Atlas Cedar

male flower

cone

bark

arching over at the tip, and usually maintains a single trunk through the conical crown. It has longer leaves than the other cedars, up to nearly 4cm long, stout and deep green. It can be seen in the gardens of Victorian houses around towns, as well as in parks and larger gardens everywhere.

The **Cyprus Cedar**, *Cedrus brevifolia*, is found only in the Troodos Mountains and is normally seen only in big collections in Britain. It has much the shortest needles of the four, and a dark grey bark of nearly square plates.

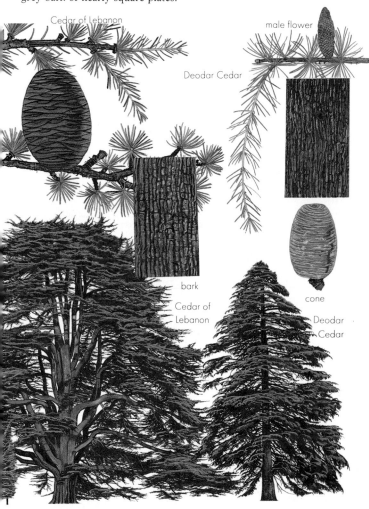

Cedar of Lebanon

male flower

Deodar Cedar

bark

Cedar of Lebanon

cone

Deodar Cedar

Larches

The **European Larch**, *Larix decidua*, is deciduous, like all other larches, its leaves turning gold before they fall in autumn. This loss of leaves is very unusual amongst conifers, only occurring elsewhere in the group in some of the Redwoods, which lose their shoots as well. The European Larch grows wild in the Alps, Tatra and Carpathian mountains. It was first grown in Britain in about 1625 and became common after extensive plantings which began in 1770. Larch comes into flower early and the leaves open soon after, but leading shoots do not expand until much later, in May. By June a strong young tree will be adding 10cm a week.

The **Japanese Larch**, *Larix kaempferi* or *L. leptolepis*, grows in central Hoshu and on Mt. Fuji. It was introduced to Britain in 1861 and was used in forestry from 1886 onwards. By 1940 wide expanses of hillsides, particularly in central Wales, were under plantations on thin bracken soils where this tree grows faster than European Larch. Its crown is more dense, the bole expands more rapidly and it casts more shade.

The hybrid between these two, the **Hybrid Larch**, *Larix* x *eurolepis*, was first recognised in 1904 in Scotland. The hybrid is intermediate between the parent species in all features except that it has more flowers and taller cones than either. It can grow faster than either on many difficult sites, for example on thin peats, in polluted air and on spoil heaps. Young trees on good soil can be 20m tall in as many years.

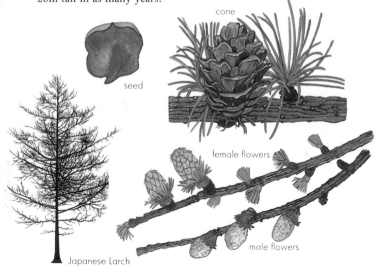

cone

seed

female flowers

male flowers

Japanese Larch

European Larch

male flowers

female flowers

seed

Hybrid Larch

seed

European Larch

Spruces

The **Norway Spruce**, *Picea abies*, ranges widely in the mountains of Europe and was growing in Britain by 1548. It is now most familiar as the Christmas Tree, but at one time was extensively planted as a forest tree, until replaced by the Sitka Spruce during this century. It grows best on north facing slopes or in deep northern glens and is quite short-lived for a conifer, few trees surviving more than 200 years. Most of the trees have a 'brush' crown, with shoots growing in all directions, but a few have a 'comb' crown, with the shoots hanging in lines from well-spaced branches.

The **Sitka Spruce**, *Picea sitchensis*, grows on offshore islands and on the mainland near the coast, from Alaska to California, in North America. The Sitka is the world's biggest spruce, reaching 93m tall on Vancouver Island. The first seeds were sent to Britain in 1831. The trees grew so well and so tall that in 1920 the Forestry Commissioners adopted Sitka as the main species for planting in the western Highlands. Even now, almost 70 years later, no tree has been found to rival it, and it is the mainstay of forest production in all the western hills.

Sitka is highly attractive in spring, with bright green brushes of foliage on blue-green and silvered crowns. It is disliked by conservationists although its new plantings are rich in bird species, especially finches and warblers.

The **Oriental Spruce**, *Picea orientalis*, from the Caucasus and northeastern Turkey, was introduced in 1839 and planted in pinetums and large gardens. It has the shortest needles of any spruce, shining dark green and growing all around the shoots.

cone

Oriental Spruce

Sitka Spruce bark

female flowers

male flowers

Norway Spruce

male flowers

Sitka Spruce

female flowers

cone

Sitka Spruce

Hemlocks

The Hemlocks are a small group of conifers related to the spruces. They are native to North America, the Himalayas, China and Japan. They are called 'hemlocks' because the crushed leaves of the Eastern Hemlock, the first known to botanists, is supposed to have a scent similar to the famous poisonous herb.

The **Western Hemlock**, *Tsuga heterophylla*, is the giant of the genus, and in Washington State, near the middle of its range from Alaska to northern California, some trees are 70m tall. The tree was introduced to Britain in 1851 and the numerous big trees in Scotland were planted in and after 1860. Young trees will grow in considerable shade and are useful for planting under old oak, larch and pine although the timber is only useful for pulp.

The Western Hemlock shares a feature of growth with the Deodar and Lawson Cypress alone among the world's trees. It dangles its leading shoot as a 'dropper' in a wide arc, an adaptation to growing up beneath other trees and threading its way through them, eventually to dominate them. The fragile new growth is always pointing downwards, out of harm's way when the woody arc of the top is blown against an adjacent branch. In the middle of the growing season, the old dropper leader straightens up, going past the offending branch and bringing the now hardened new shoot up to become the new dropper, the terminal bud still hanging below.

male flowers

immature cone

Eastern Hemlock

The **Eastern Hemlock**, *Tsuga canadensis*, is as shapely as the Western and a pale green in its native woods, from Nova Scotia to Georgia, but in Britain it is nearly always a dark, dull tree with big low branches making a low crown. Being usually bushy when young, it is occasionally planted as a hedge, but the Western Hemlock makes a better one. There are many old trees in country gardens, with coarsely-fissured, nearly black bark.

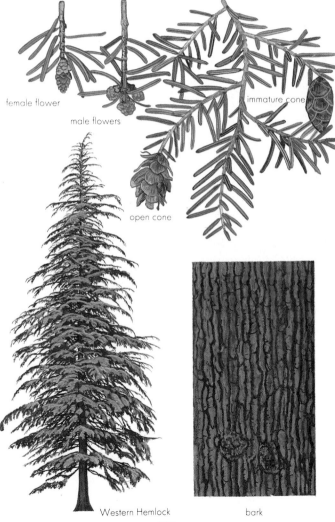

female flower

male flowers

immature cone

open cone

Western Hemlock

bark

Pines

The **Scots Pine**, *Pinus sylvestris*, has the widest range of any pine, growing from the mountains of Spain and Scotland through the Crimea to eastern Siberia. It was planted as the chief forest tree on most Scottish estates until replaced after 1850 by faster-growing American conifers. It is still favoured for planting on high ground on many Scottish estates and in Northumberland. It was the usual species for planting on English heaths, like the Breckland in Norfolk and in north Hampshire. Today in such areas the pines have run wild and thousands of seedlings are cut by conservationists each year to preserve some habitats for the rare Dartford Warblers, Natterjack Toads and Smooth Snakes.

The trees bear female flowers at the tips of the most vigorous shoots, male flowers on weak dangling shoots. The cones swell to become bright shiny green the following summer and woody and ripe by the autumn.

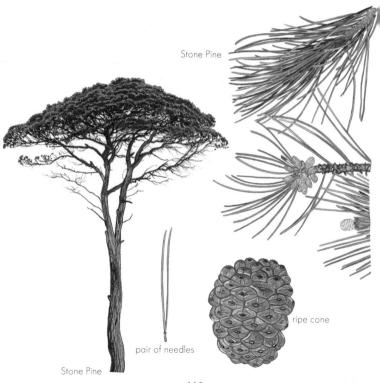

Stone Pine

pair of needles

ripe cone

Stone Pine

The **Stone Pine**, *Pinus pinea*, was probably the first exotic conifer to be grown in Britain, brought from the Mediterranean around 500 years ago. It grows well in England and southern Scotland, with many of the biggest trees on the west side, in Wales, Devon and Cornwall. The tree does not develop adult foliage until it is four or five years old; until then it forms a narrow bush, but by ten years old it is beginning to form the broad umbrella crown typical of the old tree. It has big seeds which are made into flour in Italy, and eaten raw or cooked in many other countries.

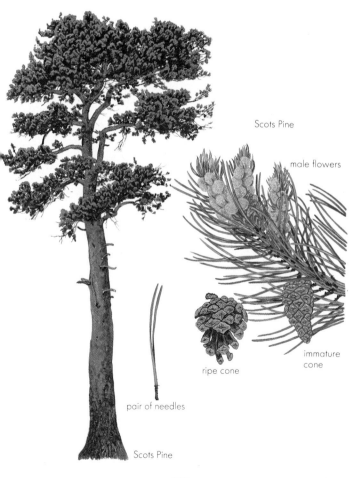

Scots Pine

male flowers

immature cone

ripe cone

pair of needles

Scots Pine

Pines

The **Austrian Pine**, *Pinus nigra* var. *nigra*, is the Black Pine of central Europe and was not grown in Britain until 1840. It is now very common, in shelterbelts and around old gardens in suburbs, on railway embankments, in town parks and near the sea and is an exceptionally tough tree for planting on difficult soils like chalk, clay or sand. It has the blackest, scaliest, most rugged bark of all the Black Pines and the shortest, most curved and stiffest needles.

The **Corsican Pine**, *Pinus nigra* var. *maritima*, is the form of Black Pine found in Corsica and southern Italy. It was the first of the Black Pines to be introduced into Britain, in 1729, and the only one important in forestry. It is an unusually useful conifer since it grows on chalk, clay and poor sands and is highly resistant to pollution. Today it is replacing Scots Pine on many southern heaths and in the Norfolk Brecklands because it yields timber in much greater volume. It is common in shelterbelts and around gardens, like the Austrian Pine, but has a superior shape with more open, lax foliage. The needles are very long and twisted. Great Spotted Woodpeckers will take cones to an old stump to extract the seeds, building up piles of discards.

The **Lodgepole Pine**, *Pinus contorta*, comes from western North America where it has two distinct forms, the inland Lodgepole Pine, var. *latifolia* and the Shore Pine, var. *contorta*, from the Pacific coast. Both are abundant in this country in extensive upland forest plantations, mostly planted since 1950, and with the Shore

Austrian Pine

cone

Pine predominating. The Shore Pine has a dense crown with strong, low branches and a curved stem at the base; with time it forms a dense, broad dome. The Lodgepole Pine has a straight stem but it has not been a great success because its thin, light foliage does not suppress heather and it tends to fork repeatedly. Both forms flower within a few years of being planted and they retain the short-prickled cones in great numbers for years.

Corsican Pine

Lodgepole Pine

ripe cone

cone

Shore Pine

bark

Corsican Pine

Pines

The **Maritime Pine**, *Pinus pinaster*, from the western
Mediterranean was introduced at an early, unknown date, like the
Stone Pine. It grows north to the Scottish Highlands in Britain,
and the biggest specimens are in the Midlands and southeastern
England. Most of them are hidden deep in estates in Sussex. There
are a few plantations, however, near the sea and on sand dunes, and
they have an unmistakeable aspect with swept bases to the boles
and very open canopies. The cones adhere in clusters for many
years and when picked newly ripe they are ornamental, shining rich
red-brown, and up to 12cm long. Its needles are the stoutest of all
those borne in pairs.

The **Arolla Pine**, *Pinus cembra*, is a five-needle pine with
densely-held foliage and a level-branched columnar crown. Its
cones, deep blue in summer, are borne only rather high on old trees
and fall complete with seeds. It is planted high in the Swiss Alps,
to hold back the snow on slopes liable to avalanches and is
reasonably common in all parts of Britain in small numbers.

The **Monterey Pine**, *Pinus radiata*, comes from the Carmel
peninsular in California, where, infested by a brown and lethal
mistletoe, it barely reaches 23m tall and tends to die at around 100
years old. Yet only 90km north, in San Francisco, planted trees can
grow 16m tall in five years. In this country, it is found in many old
gardens in the south and west from Kent to Argyll, and in Ireland.
In the semi-tropics it grows continuously without setting a bud and
is the mainstay of many timber industries.

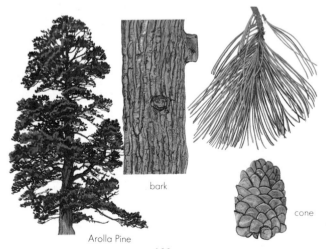

bark

cone

Arolla Pine

The Monterey Pine is a fire-climax tree, holding on to its cones until a fire comes through the crown. In the general absence of such fires in Britain, the cones remain unopened for 20 years or more, their weight often causing a branch to come down. Cones wrested from a branch can be put into a hot oven and the seeds will be expelled and grow well; they transplant poorly however. They grow fast on any soil, even on chalk but in that case they turn yellow when about 30 years old and soon deteriorate.

Maritime Pine

male flowers

female flowers

cone

Monterey Pine

cone

Monterey Pine

Maritime Pine

PRACTICAL
REFERENCE
SECTION

Suitable Trees for the Garden

The following tables contain a wide range of trees and are not confined to those that are only appropriate for small gardens. Some will grow very large indeed, and these are indicated by (L) in the 20-year height column. Those trees that will never make large spreading specimens are marked (S).

The list is, however, limited to the more desirable trees, with an emphasis on year-round features, bark and shape, and foliage. The use of the common English names creates a few infelicities like the incense cedar among the true cedars, and the southern beeches scattered under 'Beech', 'Dombey's', 'Rauli' and 'Roble'. The fancy Japanese cherries are so numerous that they have been combined under 'Sato' cherry, and their details generalized.

Height after ten years is bedevilled by the deplorable range in the size of plants sold, but evens itself out somewhat since trees planted when two or three metres tall will not grow, while 60cm plants grow fast. Standard trees unavoidably start at over two metres and so grow slowly.

'Spread' is a loose concept and varies according to individual characteristics as well as the space available. The figures given are for 20-year old, average shaped trees growing in the open.

Key
B   Broadleaf
C   Conifer
L   Trees grow to a large size
S   Trees that remain relatively small

Common Name	Height after 20 years (metres)	Spread (metres)	Good Features	Failings
Alder, Italian (B)	15–20 (L)	6	Vigour, catkins, shape, foliage	No autumn colours
Apple (B)				
Hupeh crab	12	6–8	Vigour, flower, fruit	
Japanese crab	4–7 (S)	5–8	Unfailingly floriferous	Low, densely twiggy crown
Pillar	10–15	3	Shape, new foliage, autumn colour	
Ash (B)				
Caucasian/Claret	10–17	6–8	Bark, bright elegant foliage	
Manna	7–12	5	Flowers, scent	
Beech (B)				
Dawyck	14–17	2–3	Shape, spring and autumn colour	
Birch (B)				
Fastiagiate	10–15	1–2	Bark, shape	Can become untidy
Swedish	14–18	2–4	Bark, crown, foliage	
Transcaucasian	5–6 (S)	5–6	Crown, foliage, autumn colour	Low and rather slow
Catalpa (B)				
Hybrid	10–12	5–7	Foliage, flower	Short season, gaunt
Northern	10–12	4–5	Foliage, flower	Short season
Cedar (C)				
Blue Atlas	12–15 (L)	8–10	Vigour, colour	Spreads with age
Incense	12–14 (L)	2	Crown, colour	

Common Name	Height after 20 years (metres)	Spread (metres)	Good Features	Failings
Cherry (B)				
Bird	5–6 (S)	3–5	Flower, autumn colour	Coarse foliage, poor crown
Japanese 'Sato'	4–10 (S)	1–5	Flower, autumn colour	
'Pandora'	9–10 (S)	2–3	Flower, autumn colour	
Sargent	9–12	3–6	Flower, autumn colour	
Wild	15–18 (L)	3–5	Vigour, flower, autumn colour	Suckering roots
Winter	5–8 (S)	3–7	Six months of flower	Twiggy, sprawling crown
Chestnut (B)				
Indian horse-	12–14 (S)	4–6	Opening leaf, flower, foliage	Shape needs watching
Japanese horse-	9–13	4–5	Huge foliage, flowers autumn colour	
Cypress (C)				
Smooth Arizona	10–14	3–4	Any soil; shape, colour, tough	
Cripp's Golden	5–8	5–6	Shape, colour	Green forms dull
Leyland	17–20 (L)	5–6	Vigour, shape, tough	
Dove-tree (B)	6–12	4–6	Flower, foliage, interest	Rather gaunt when leafless
Fir (C)				
Grand	15–20 (L)	4–5	Vigour, shape, height	Not in dry or much exposure
Korean	3–6 (S)	2	Flowers, cones, shape	Usually bushy, slow
Gingko (C)	5–8	2–3	Interest, shape, foliage	Unreliable shape and growth
Gum (B)				
Cider	15–20	5–9	Vigour, bark, foliage, flowers	Liable to blow when young
Snow	12–18	3–5	Bark, new leaves, foliage, flowers	Variable bark and growth

Name			Features	Notes
Mountain	6–10	2–3	Shape, colour, tough	Best in wet west, and north
Western	10–18 (L)	3–4	Shape, vigour, clay or sand	Poor in east, dry, towns
Honeylocust (B)	8–12	4–6	Foliage, autumn colour, dry	Needs heat, short season
Judas tree (B)	6–8 (S)	3–5	Foliage, flower, autumn colour	Slow, reclines with age, fragile
Katsura tree (B)	9–14	4–7	Vigour, shape, foliage, autumn colour	Resents late frost and drought
Keaki (B)	7–10	5–8	Shape, foliage, autumn bark	May spread when young
Laburnum, Voss's (B)	9–10 (S)	2–4	Flower	Poor thing for 50 weeks
Larch, European (C)	12–17 (L)	3–5	Vigour, early and late colour	
Lime (B)				
Cutleaf	8–10	3–4	Shape, foliage, flower	
Silver	12–15 (L)	4–6	Vigour, shape, flower, towns	With age sprouty and burrs
Small-leaf	9–12 (L)	3–5	Foliage, flower	
Madrone (B)	9–13 (S)	3–5	Foliage, bark, flowers	May be short lived
Magnolia (B)				
Veitch's	9–12	4–7	Flowers early in life	Coarse foliage
Willow	8–9 (S)	4–5	Shape, foliage, flower	
Maple (B)				
Ashleaf	11–12	5–6	Cultivars – foliage	Revert to green, short life
Japanese (Downy)	4–8 (S)	1–3	Foliage, flower, autumn colour	
(Smooth)	3–6 (S)	3–5	Foliage, shape, autumn colour	Variable growth
Norway	12–15 (L)	4–5	Flower, autumn, colour	
Silver	12–20 (L)	6–10	Vigour, foliage, size	Brittle high branches
Snakebarks	8–12 (S)	6–9	Bark, foliage, autumn, colour	Spreading upper crown

Common Name	Height after 20 years (metres)	Spread (metres)	Good Features	Failings
Monkey-puzzle (C)	5–12	3–5	Character, foliage, contrast	Slow to start, harsh litter
Mulberry (B)				
Black (Seedling)	2–4	2–3	Shape, foliage, fruit	Slow to start, fruit mess paths
(Truncheon)	3–5	3–5		
Oak (B)				
Common	9–12 (L)	3–6	Wildlife, character, autumn colour	Galled, often sprouty
Red	12–15 (L)	6–8	Vigour, new foliage,	Variable autumn colours
Sessile	11–14 (L)	5–7	Vigour, shape, foliage	
Paulownia (B)	12–15	5–7	Flowers, foliage	Short life and season
Redwood (C)				
Coast	12–18 (L)	3–6	Vigour, interest	Browns in cold dry winds
Dawn	10–17	3–5	Interest, foliage, shape, autumn colour	Needs moist site
Rowan (B)				
Hupeh	10–12 (S)	3–5	Foliage, fruit	Grafts sprout at base
Scarlet	9–11 (S)	4–7	Foliage, fruit, autumn colour	
Vilmorin	5–7	5–8	Foliage, fruit, autumn colour	Low, spreading, slow
Sequoia, Giant (C)	12–17 (L)	4–5	Size, shape	Often struck by lightning
Snowbell tree (B)	6–8	4–6	Flower, shape	
Spruce (C)				
Blue Colorado	6–10	2–3	Colour, shape	Spruce aphid, red spider
Brewer	5–6	2–3	Shape	Seedlings best, but slow start
Serbian	10–13	3	Shape, tolerance soil, town	Susceptible to honey fungus

Name	Height	Spread	Features	Notes
Sweetgum (B)	9–12	3–4	Foliage, autumn colour	Variable colour, needs good soil
Thorn (B)				
Carrière's	7–8 (S)	4–6	Flowers, fruit, tolerance	Possibly fireblight
Plumleaf	5–8 (S)	4–6	Foliage, autumn colour	Bushy unless legged
Tulip tree (B)	9–15 (L)	3–6	Foliage, autumn colour, flowers	Best with warm summers
Tupelo (B)	5–10	2–4	Autumn colour	Slow, needs warm rich site
Walnut (B)				
Black	8–13 (L)	3–5	Vigour, shape foliage, autumn colour	Needs deep rich soil, warmth
Common	9–12	4–6	New and summer foliage, fruit	Needs deep rich soil, sun
Whitebeam (B)	10–12 (S)	3–4	Foliage, flowers, fruit	Birds eat fruit
Willow (B)				
Bay	7–10 (S)	2–5	Foliage, flower	Needs cool, damp site
Corkscrew	10–15	5–6	Interest, early and late foliage	Prone to anthracnose disease
Weeping	10–15	8–12	Shape, early foliage	Prone to disease, thirsty roots
Yew (C)				
Common	4–6	2–4	Dark background, immortal	Slow
Irish	3–5 (S)	1–2	Shape	Slow, dull in numbers
Wingnut (B)				
Hybrid	15–18 (L)	6–9	Vigour, foliage, autumn colour	Suckers luxuriantly
Zelkova, Caucasian (B)	10–12 (L)	4–7	Foliage, autumn colour	May turn out ordinary shape

Planting a Tree

Preparing the Hole

Nearly all trees make more reliable, sturdy growth in their first few years if they are transplanted, than if seed is sown and the plants left undisturbed. Nevertheless it is a wholly unnatural break in its growth pattern for a tree to be planted – one to which it cannot have evolved a response – and the operation should be planned to cause the least possible disruption to growth. The crucial point is to make the move as early in the tree's life as possible, to allow it the formative first five or six years in its final position. The bigger and older a tree is when planted, the more its growth is retarded, the longer it takes to make the big root system it needs for growth and stability. A tree three metres tall is easily crippled for life by being moved, and no tree so big should even be considered for purchase unless it has a big root system prepared over several years in the nursery.

The best size for planting is 30–40cm, from open ground or a large container, where the roots have never been cramped. Such a plant, with all its roots, planted firmly, is stable from the start, must not be staked and will grow away rapidly to build a stout bole and shapely crown. A tall plant has already made its lower crown in response to conditions in the nursery lines, and so it will be drawn up with a slender, weak stem, often made worse by being tied to a stake. For a healthy plant, the stem must grow in the place where the tree is to spend its life and in response to the surroundings there. The foliage of a tree feeds its roots and the roots feed the foliage. A tree planted out usually has less shelter than in a nursery and its foliage is under more stress from drying winds. So it needs a vigorous root system. With the usual tiny, cramped incomplete one of a tall plant it can scarcely leaf out at all, much less make new shoots. So there are few leaves to feed the roots during their vital time for expansion into new soil. Thus, little growth can be made on the roots, and little on shoots; the tree is locked into a stage of minimum growth and has a dire struggle to survive, for many years.

A small plant with almost natural rooting evades this trap. Roots must be spread out to reach the new soil, not left in a ball. Pot-bound roots must be at least partially unravelled even if some break and need to be cut back. The size of hole needed can then be seen – big enough to take the spread roots with a small margin extra. The bottom of the hole is dug out to allow 15cm of good soil or leaf mould beneath the tree, and the base well broken up if it is a heavy soil. A mixture of the surrounding soil, compost and sand is put round the spread roots and gently firmed.

In poor sandy soils a little superphosphate fertilizer spread over

Preparing the Hole

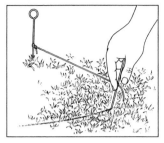

1. *A circular area of cleared ground is most suitable, and easily marked for the new tree. Swing a marker 1m from a pin.*

2. *Remove a thin top layer of turf and put it aside. Most of the good topsoil stays to be dug out and mixed to make the backfill.*

3. *Break up the bottom of the hole well, if it is compacted, to provide good drainage. If it is good loam, it can just be dug over.*

4. *Break up the turf taken from the top and put it at the bottom of the hole, where it will break down into good rooting soil.*

5. *Spread a layer of well-rotted manure, leaf mould or compost over the turves to conserve moisture and allow easy rooting.*

6. *Firm in the bottom layers before the tree roots are put in place, to ensure that there are no pockets of air in the lower layers.*

Planting the tree

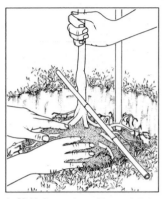

1. *Hold the tree in position and shake it up and down gently, as soil is spread around and among the roots.*

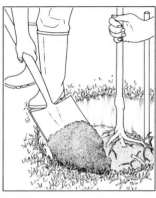

2. *Using a cane to mark the soil level, hold the tree while filling the hole to old level and firming.*

3. *Tread the top firm; then lightly fork the surface to break it up slightly to allow in water and air.*

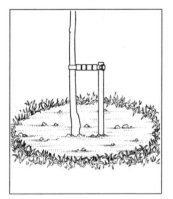

4. *Trees should be provided with a short stake to hold them still until the roots have grown.*

the bottom before placing the tree in the hole aids rapid root-growth; while some slow-release nitrogenous fertilizer like bonemeal added to the backfill improves early shoot growth.

The level of the surface on the stem before planting can be seen, and filling brings the new soil to the same place; then after heavy firming it is made good to that level again. In light soils the new tree and a 1m radius around is left 10cm below the surrounding level; the tree needs frequent watering and the water then stays around the tree.

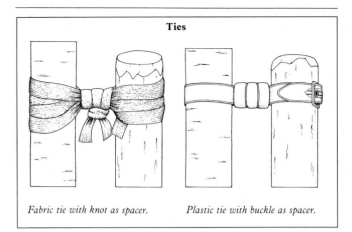

Ties

Fabric tie with knot as spacer. *Plastic tie with buckle as spacer.*

Staking and Tying

Standard and other large trees need a stake, not to hold the stem up but just to hold it still until the new roots have grown. After that it is bad for the tree to be staked, as it needs to sway to grow its proper, stout stem. A short strong stake, firmly set 30cm away holds a tie on the bole 30cm away from the ground and is removed after the second growing season and the winter gales. A large tree from a container is best held by a triangle of three short stakes, because driving one into the root ball would very likely damage important roots. (One stake each side is adequate for trees of moderate size).

Stakes should not be longer than is needed to hold the ties at 30cm. Projecting into the crown they can damage branches and serve no purpose, unless sometimes in public places, they lessen vandal damage. The heaviest standards with big tops may need their support at one third of the height of their stems.

Stakes should be long enough to allow them to be buried 40–60cm deep, be knot-free and straight-grained for strength. They must be free from disease, preferably tanalized or otherwise treated with preservative unless they are Western Red Cedar.

Ties must have some elasticity to allow unhindered expansion of the stem even in the two seasons at most that they are needed. They must have spacers to prevent the stake rubbing the tree and be fixed firmly, on the stake to prevent them from, slipping down in bad weather.

Pruning and Shaping

Trees normally assume their best shape in their own way. Only those grown for their fruit need annual pruning to increase the size, number or accessibility of the fruit. In the case of all other trees, the term 'pruning' has a very different meaning, covering two separate operations.

The first of these is to aid the natural process of shedding the first, lowest branches in order to give a clean, smooth bole. In woodland these are soon shaded out and shed, but on single trees the strongest branches extend into the light and keep growing at their tips while the inner shoots and smaller branches become bare. Left alone, these make a tangle of dead wood hiding the bole and soon full of nettles and rubbish, while big low branches disfigure the tree. Even where a lawn-tree is intended to be feathered to the ground, the early removal of the branch tangle on the bottom 1.5m allows the next layer to drop around a clean bole. Other trees can have 2m of clean stem by the time they are 6m tall.

The second operation − shaping − is required only to rectify a fault in growth. A forking leading shoot can be singled as soon as it is seen. A forked, two-stem tree is ugly and vulnerable to storms. Misplaced or over-vigorously protruding branches should be removed when necessary.

Where to cut

Removing side branches from a stem early in its life, when they are only a few centimetres in diameter, can be done at any time of year. The small scars which are left close in a year or two, leaving a smooth stem. Removing older stems and taking branches from the crown leaves big scars. Branches usually swell out at their origin to a conic protrusion. This causes conflict between two desired aims − a minimum size of scar and a cut flush with the major stem or branch to leave it smooth. Controversy raged for 400 years and decay followed pruning whether the cut was flush, left a marked stub or if a rough unreasoned compromise was made. Dr A. Shigo of New Hampshire has shown exactly where the cuts should be made and why.

The Shigo Method

In beech alone there was an old method of pruning small branches leaving a 5cm stub. Coral-spot fungus was sure to infect this but by the time it reached the main stem, the tree had sealed off the scar and the stub would fall off with the fungus to leave a healed scar. Were the cut flush with the bole the fungus could have entered the stem and decayed a large, deep scar.

Dr Shigo has shown that *all* trees isolate areas of decay with barriers of resistant cells; that the junctions of branches have the tissues for growing the barriers already disposed in a pattern to prepare for natural shedding, and he has described how these show on the tree. A 'branch bark ridge' on the upper side and a 'branch collar' on the underside mark the outer rim of tissues that will grow the barrier, which is conical, pointing inwards.

The natural death of a branch causes the collar to enlarge. When the branch is decayed and breaks off it will tend to take with it the conical insertion. However if this remains and rots, it is isolated from the main stem, and the exterior is sealed in by growth from the enlarged collar. The cut must be close to but clear of the collar.

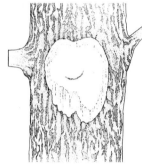

The Wrong Way *Cutting flush with the stem leaves a smooth surface, but the branch is thickest at the base so such a cut leaves a bigger scar. Worse, this cut removes the collar of tissues whose function is to heal the scar, so the wound heals slowly. Few dressings inhibit decay and many make a skin which cracks and lets water lodge against the scar. Unless repainted often, dressings thus encourage decay. The correct cut leaves the collar intact to close the scar.*

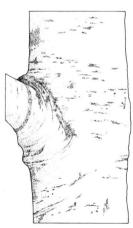

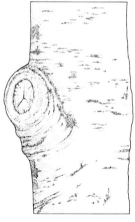

The Right Way *The correct cut is from just clear of the 'branch bark ridge' above to just clear of the collar below. The collar may not show; then the angle of the cut is shown by the* angle that the ridge makes away from the branch. The cut is at the same angle from the vertical in the opposite direction.

Singling a Fork

A symmetrical fork in new growth on a very young tree may be left until new growth begins next season

but no longer. Unequal forks may call for a choice between a weak shoot and a strong one that is more offset.

Singling Sprouts

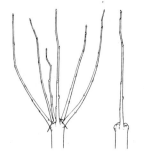 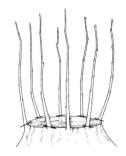

A eucalypt or similar tree may regrow after a hard frost as many shoots from ground level. Choose one strong shoot and cut the others.

A sprouting stump can be regrown as a tree, cutting out all but the single strongest and most shapely new shoot.

Crown Thinning

 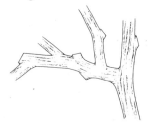

Some broadleaf trees have crowns which can become congested. Savage cutting makes them worse.

Thinning the crown by intelligent removal of excess leafage on whole branch systems, always cutting back to a main branch, cures the trouble.

Cutting	**Cleaning the Bole**

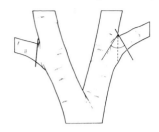

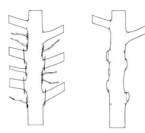

All but the lightest branches are cut to a stub before pruning, to prevent tearing. First a shallow undercut, then the full cut a few inches outside.

A bole can be cleaned when branches are 10–15cm across. Beyond that it would leave too much scar. A clean bole for 1.5m is a minimum aim.

Improving Growth of Young Trees

Trees are sociable plants and in nature they normally arise and grow in groups, either of their own species only or amongst others. Even the pioneer species – the first to colonize bare ground – usually spring up in numbers together.

The new bare sites are largely those cleared by fire (due to lightning before the arrival of man and often afterwards also) but greatly increased by deliberate burning to clear the land for grazing and crops. In western North America most of the coniferous forests have large areas of uniform age which can be dated back to a fire and most of the trees have a life-cycle adapted to the average period between fires, which itself is fixed by the time needed for enough combustible material to accumulate. Other new sites arise on a smaller scale from landslides, rivers changing course and swamps drying out. Pioneer species have light seeds, often with fluff or wings, and are carried by the wind much further than heavier fruits which are dispersed by mammals or birds, usually in established woods. The trees bearing the heavier fruits therefore come in only after the pioneers have created a form of woodland. Hence the successor species are also adapted to growing up among trees – at first those of a different species from themselves.

The aspens, poplars and willows have fluff on their seeds and are long distance pioneers. The birches with minute winged seeds can travel a fair distance, and pines, with heavy winged seeds, are usually short distance pioneers.

The first trees on new land grow in conditions very different

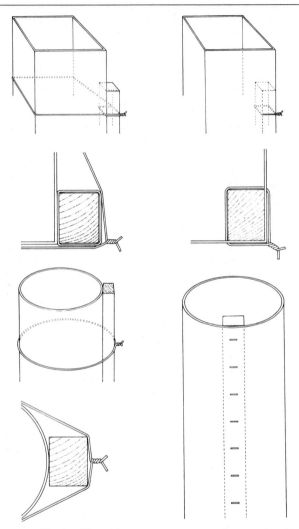

Types of Shelter *Normal Shelters are 1.2m long, square or round, and can be translucent, green or brown. They last 5 years, until degraded by sunlight. Weeds must be removed before setting up the shelter; those outside may be sprayed. Shelters must be held firmly and the base pushed into the soil. A tile batten 25mm² is driven 30cm into loam, 50cm into sand, 2cm from the stem. Galvanised mild steel wire of 16 gauge can be used to hold the shelter to the batten. If the batten is softwood, staples may be used.*

from those found in woodlands. There will be open sky and either newly formed soil or newly burned surfaces. If new, the soil will usually be short of the nutrients needed for growth, particularly in nitrogen, and lacking entirely in humus. If burned, it will also lack nitrogen but be high in potash, and the top at least will lack humus. So pioneer species need to adapt to poor, often open, sandy soils and to have a low demand for nutrients. But the overwhelming factor on new exposed sites is the wind which causes the soil, at best open and poor in humus, to dry out rapidly. Pioneer trees must be able to withstand drought. They can do so by early development of wide, deep roots and by having small or thick-skinned leaves.

Small tough leaves or dense hairs on shoots and leaves lessen the damaging drying effect of the wind on the foliage. Big thin leaves can be grown only by trees whose entire life is spent in the shelter of old woods. The pioneer trees have no need of dense foliage to catch enough light, since they grow in open places. Their leaves work only in nearly full light, and are shed when they become shaded by others and the crowns remain light and open. This allows the wind to filter through where a dense crown would be damaged by strong gusts. It also allows strong growth of the early arrivals among the ground herbs, and later the growth of the more shade-bearing trees that will take over when the pioneers have created shelter and their leaf fall has built up a much improved soil.

The pioneers make rapid early growth, flower and fruit within a few years of germinating from seed and tend to be short-lived. These qualities are further adaptations to their life-style. They do need, however, to modify the severity of their surroundings in order to grow well, or, in the more extreme sites, to grow at all. This can be done only by growing in large numbers together from the start, which is the normal result of seeding on to bare ground. Each tree then benefits from the shelter of the others and this common shelter increases as the trees grow and improves greatly the microclimate within the stand. Even the trees on the periphery benefit, since the trees behind retard the wind that sweeps through them. Height growth increases with distance from the edge.

The pioneer stands are usually fairly open, but there are exceptions such as the birch tracts following heath fires and the Lodgepole Pine stands in the interior Rocky Mountains, which arise and largely remain in very dense groups, despite a high rate of suppression and death.

Successor species are adapted to starting life in the sheltered, relatively humid conditions of woodlands, in a humus-rich, reasonably fertile soil. Many need open sky above them after varying periods and achieve this end either by outgrowing the species around them or by biding their time until the canopies above them fail and fall with age.

The conclusions to be drawn from all these factors is that a tree,

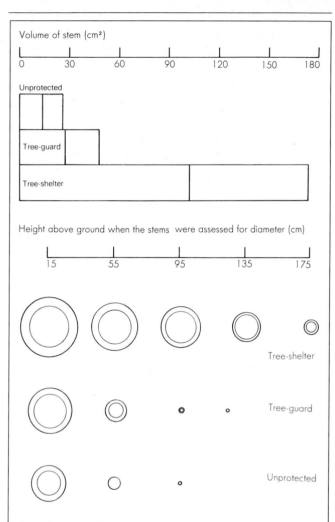

Volume of stem (cm²)

| 0 | 30 | 60 | 90 | 120 | 150 | 180 |

Unprotected

Tree-guard

Tree-shelter

Height above ground when the stems were assessed for diameter (cm)

| 15 | 55 | 95 | 135 | 175 |

Tree-shelter

Tree-guard

Unprotected

Growth Comparisons: 3 and 4 years Oak. *60 trees. 20 control (unprotected); 20 with tree-guard (plastic net); and 20 with tree-shelter.*
TOP. *Volume of stems. Unshaded portion; third year: shaded portion; fourth year.*
BOTTOM. *The same trees, mean cross-sections at 40cm intervals up the stems. Inner disc; size after 3 years; outer ring, growth in fourth year. Trees in shelters increase in stem volume in their third year as much as those in tree guards had increased in their four years from the acorn. Silver Birch, Norway Maple, Sycamore etc reacted similarly.*

of any kind, either planted singly or widely spaced on an open site as in most amenity plantings in parks or around buildings, faces conditions from which its natural manner of growth largely shields it. To make matters worse, it is usually planted out when it is far too big, and has spent too many years in the very different conditions of the nursery. The worst aspect for the tree is the sudden subjection to exposure.

Tuley Tubes

Graham Tuley of the Forestry Commission experimented with translucent plastic 'tree shelters' of different materials, widths and heights. A narrow shelter gives a 'greenhouse effect', retaining within it the heat it receives from radiated light – an effect that is apparent if you put your hand into one on a cool day. In the calm damp warmth the side shoots grow big leaves which promote growth in the stem and leading shoot. They are short and congested but are removed when the stem is cleaned up. The shelter also protects the tree from damage by animals. Growth in many broadleaf trees is given a rapid early start, most spectacularly in oaks but all species tested have benefited when provided with shelters. Among conifers, only Japanese Larch responds strongly. Some trees, notably oaks, cannot hold up the big crown that results. They must be secured to the stake that held the shelter when the plastic has degraded away after the expected five years. Over 500,000 Tuley tubes were used in one year in Great Britain.

Measuring Height

The height of a tree less than about 6m tall can be measured
accurately with a rod. The height of a tall tree can also be measured
reasonably closely but exact measurement of its height is normally
impracticable. Even climbing the tree can rarely solve the problem.
The path for the tape down the bole cannot be direct, the precise
tip cannot be seen by the climber or judged accurately, and the tree
may lean.

Height is reckoned from the highest point of the crown and this
may be, in an old many-headed conifer or a broad, domed broadleaf
tree, many metres from the central axis. Its position has to be
decided from a distance and the point directly beneath it estimated
from under the crown. The bottom of a tree is the highest point to
which soil reaches up the bole. This prevents the extended bole and
roots on the downhill side of a steep slope from counting in the
height.

Having observed the points between which the measurement is to
be made, the next thing to decide is the place from which to make
it. Accuracy is best at a distance from the tree which is equal to its
height and from the same level as its base. A rough estimate of the
height of the tree − 20, 30 or 40m − is made and a position found
at about the equivalent distance as nearly level with the base as
possible, from which the top and bottom can be seen. A leaning
tree is sighted at a right-angle to the direction of the lean if
possible.

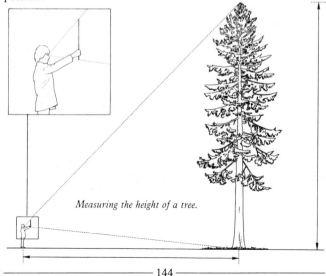

Measuring the height of a tree.

Estimating Age

The height and spread of a tree both increase with age until senility begins and then they decrease again. Both fail as indicators of age beyond the early years. Diameter and bole circumference increase every year of life, a ring of new wood being added annually. The circumference, measured at 1.5m, is a good guide to age.

For big-growing trees (not those like apples and holly) the broad rule of roughly 2.5cm increase in circumference applies regardless of species, region or altitude, over a wide span of years. Most trees add well over 2cm a year in youth and gradually decline first to 2cm and then to less. In an old tree the increase is on or close to 2cm per year over a very long period. Wood added depends on the amount of foliage, so a tree crowded in a wood or having lost branches adds less each year and may fit 2cm every two years. A fully crowned oak 6m around will usually be about 250 years old.

There are, however, both hares and tortoises among trees. Fast growth, that is 7 – 10cm a year, is made each year by the best eucalypts, willows and poplars, also by Giant Sequoias, Coast Redwoods, Dawn Redwoods and some Grand Firs.

A few trees grow more than 2cm a year for less than 100 years and then slow down. Examples are Scots Pine, Norway Spruce, Sycamore and Common Lime. Approximate age for these trees when their circumference is more than 2.5m, is 100 years plus an extra year for every extra 1cm.

Gilbert White recorded the Selborne Yew to be 23ft round at 3ft up in 1789. In 1984 it was 25ft 7 in (7.8m) at the same point. This would make it about 1200 years old in White's day, 1400 years old today.

Notable Tree Collections

Abbreviations

BC   Borough Council
CC   County Council
DoE   Department of the Environment
FC   Forestry Commission
NT   National Trust
NTS   National Trust of Scotland

Some National Trust properties have seasonal opening times. Many open only in the afternoon. Other properties are open either seasonally or on certain days, and details need to be ascertained from appropriate annual publications. Ownership and opening policies are always liable to change and the current position should be checked before a visit.

England
South-east

BERKSHIRE

Windsor Great Park (*HM the Queen*): Extensive plantings, conifer and broadleaf, Obelisk Pond, Totempole Ride, Botany Bay. Cyprus cedars, Limber and ponderosa pines, old coast redwoods, rare birches, maples and rowans
   Savill Garden: Metasequoia, southern beeches, bigleaf magnolia, Serbian spruce
   Valley Gardens: Magnolias, maples

Whiteknights Park (*University of Reading*): Old Turner Lucombe and cypress oaks – shagbark hickory. Recent varied planting

HAMPSHIRE AND ISLE OF WIGHT

Blackwater Arboretum, off Rhinefield Drive (*FC*): 1960 planting of great variety of conifers, a few hardwoods

Bolderwood Arboretum, nr Lyndhurst (*FC*): Huge 1859 conifers; noble fir, Hartweg pine, Crimean pine, Thuja, stand of Douglas fir (46m top height)

Broadlands, Romsey (*Lord and Lady Romsey*): Outstanding swamp cypress, good northern catalpa, horse chestnut, cedars, ginkgo

Exbury Gardens, Beaulieu (*Mr E. I. de Rothschild*): Prickly castor-oil tree, Farrer's spruce, Chinese tulip-tree, snakebark, maples, Brewer spruce

Hackwood Park, Basingstoke (*Lord Camrose*): Sugar maple, giant sequoias, Norway spruce. Adjacent to:

Herriard Park, Basingstoke (*Mr Jervoise*): Short avenue of 1851 conifers, big limes, sugar maples, Daimyo oaks, dove-trees

Hillier Arboretum, Ampfield (*Hampshire CC*): Founded 1954 to grow every species that climate and availability allow. Crabs and cherries in flower but remarkable assemblage of extreme rarities

Jenkyn Place, Bentley (*Mr and Mrs G. E. Coke*): 1823 Lebanon cedar, paperback maple, Cyprus strawberry-tree, Judas tree

Leigh Park, Havant (*Public park*): Huge tulip-tree, good fernleaf beech, giant sequoia, Kentucky coffee-tree, yellow buckeye

Longstock Gardens, Stockbridge (*John Lewis Partnership*): Wide range of species and ages. Good cherries

Osborne House, Isle of Wight (*Royal Parks*): Fine old conifers and some hardwoods. Lucombe oak avenue. Open April-October, weekdays

Rhinefield Ornamental Drive, nr Lyndhurst (*FC, public road*): 1859 background Douglas firs with mixed conifers. Outstanding Lawson cypress, Spanish fir, white spruce, giant sequoia, white pines. 1955 avenue of coast redwoods

Stratfield Saye, nr Swallowfield (*Trustees of the Duke of Wellington*): Outstanding Bosnian pines, sweetgum, Hungarian oaks, fine Metasequoias, Lebanon cedars, giant sequoias, Chinese sweetgum, in arboreta each side of House. Open spring-autumn daily

Ventnor Botanic Garden, Isle of Wight: Recent planting of a wide variety of tender trees among old pines and cypresses

KENT

Dunorlan Park, Tunbridge Wells (*Public park*): Fine deodars, ponderosa pine

Howletts Park Zoo, nr Canterbury (*Mr J. Aspinall*): Vast sweet chestnut, tallest Huntingdon elms, female ginkgo

Knole Park, Sevenoaks (*NT*): Parkland hardwoods, fine sessile oaks, beech. Garden with some conifers

Ladham House, Goudhurst (*Lady Betty Jessel*): Outstanding Metasequoia, good magnolias, mixed conifers, flowering trees

Mote Park, Maidstone (*Public park*): Huge beech, black walnut (in field), cucumber-trees, good honeylocust, Chinese elm

National Pinetum, Bedgebury, Goudhurst (*FC*): World's most comprehensive collection of conifers. Main plantings 1925–6, constant additions. Species and cultivars. Forest plots conifer and broadleaf. Some rare maples, oaks. Always open

Sandling Park, Hythe (*Mr A. Hardy*): Some fine old conifers, many younger trees, fine Dombey's beech, Monterey pine, weeping and fernleaf beeches

LONDON

Battersea Park (*Public park*): Huge collection of rare hardwoods. Hybrid horse chestnuts, Italian alders, Kentucky coffee-trees, Lobel maples, outstanding black walnut

Cannizaro Park, Wimbledon (*Public park*): Outstanding sassafrase, fine nettle-trees, maple collection, unusual oaks, good Metasequoias, tupelo, poplars

Dulwich Park and environs (*Public park*): Many fine and unusual hardwoods, swamp cypresses

Greenwich Park (*Public park*): Fine paper birch, old sweet chestnuts, shagbark hickory, gingko, Metasequoia, Kentucky coffee-tree, prickly castor-oil trees

Holland Park (*Public park*): Suttner plane, bur oak and honeylocust, yellow buckeye, pin oak, Californian laurel, Pyrenean oak, manna ash, catalpas

City of Westminster Cemetery, Uxbridge road, W7: Rare maples, birches, fine Hungarian and water oaks. Open daily

Gunnersbury Park, Ealing (*Public park*): Outstanding Daimyo oak, California laurel, Pawyck beeches

Hyde Park/Kensington Gardens (*Royal Parks*): Extensive plantings of unusual hardwoods. Outstanding manna ash, pin oak, group of single-leaf and Veltheim ashes, fine Zelvokas, wingnut, etc.

Kenwood, Hampstead (*Public park*): Fine swamp cypress, sessile oak, beeches, big old Zelkova, fine poplars red oak, London plane

Marble Hill Park, Twickenham (*Public park*): Black walnut, Italian alder, big London planes, bat willows, Cappadocian maples, red oaks

Osterley Park (*NT, Public park*): Outstanding Diamyo, Hungarian and blackjack oaks, fine sweetgums, maples, poplars,

Crimean lime, shagbark hickories, scarlet and pin oaks, small pinetum

Primrose Hill (*Royal Parks*): Fine single-leaf ash in numbers, big thorns, Crimean limes

Regent's Park (*Royal Parks*): Wide collection of mostly young, unusual hardwoods; Indian horse chestnut, Caucasian ash, fine large Oregon ash, big whitebeams, Zelkova

St James's Park (*Royal Parks*): Big catalpas, an 'Augustine Henry' London plane, euodias, cherries, thorns, swamp cypresses, Italian maples, Crimean limes

Syon Park Gardens, Brentford (*The Duke of Northumberland*): Outstanding Chinese catalpa, Zelkovas, Hungarian and swamp white oaks, swamp cypresses, Turkish hazels. Many fine rare oaks, maples. Open daily

Victoria Park, Hackney (*Public park*): Many unusual hardwoods. Washington thorn, yellow buckeyes, narrowleaf ash, Oregon maple, Zelkova

Waterlow Park, Highgate (*Public park*): Fine black walnuts, Paulownia, catalpas, wingnut

SURREY

Albury Park, Guildford (*Mutual Household Association*): Fine London planes, Corsican pine, Bhutan pines, Monterey pine, outstanding Zelkova. Open May-September, Wednesdays and Thursdays p.m.

Naphill Nurseries, near Woking (*Mr M. Slocock*): Oustanding original weeping beeches, pond cypress, willow oak, fine swamp cypress, cypress oak, Jeffrey pine

Mosses Wood, Leith Hill (*NT, public road*): Fine big conifers, Nootka and Swara cypresses, sequoias, Norway spruce, Hinoki cypress

Nonsuch Park, Epsom (*Public park*): Fine gingko, blackpines, southern magnolias in garden. Several big hardwoods outside, horse chestnut. Garden within usually open

Ramster, Chiddingfold (*Mr and Mrs P. Gunn*): Some fine hardwoods and conifers, big Colorado blue spruces, blue Atlas cedars, incense cedars, dove-tree. Open May weekends and Wednesdays p.m.

Royal Botanic Garden, Kew (*Trustees of Royal Botanic Garden*): Unrivalled collections of oaks, beech, ash, hickories, etc.

Outstanding chestnut-leafed oak, Maryland poplar, original gingko, large pinetum, golden larch

Winkworth Arboretum, Godalming (*NT*): Big collections of whitebeans and rowans, maples, oaks, fine southern beeches, line of tupelos and blue Atlas cedars, magnolias, eucryphias, madrone, hybrid wingnut

Wisley Garden, Ripley (*Royal Horticultural Society*): Notable Metasequoias, cherries, apple and maples. Extensive pinetum. Open daily except Sundays a.m.

SUSSEX

Alexandra Park, Hastings (*Public park*): Long valley including Bohemia Park and Thorpe Wood. Fine rare oaks (1880 planting), maples, varieties of beech, fine wingnuts, poplars, cherries, alders, eucalypts, cypresses

Beauport Park, Battle (*Public park and golf course*): Miles of hills and valleys of beech and oak studded with collections of rare oaks, maples, etc. Scatter of huge giant sequoias, coast redwoods, Monterey cypresses and monkey-puzzles. Outstanding silver pendent lime, Crimean pine, giant sequoia (Ring Wood)

Borde Hill, Haywards Heath (*Mr R. Clarke*): Garden and Warren Wood. Great variety of rare trees. Outstanding California laurel, Chinese stuartia, magnolias. Park and many woods abound in rarities. Collections of maples, birches, spruces, etc. Open daily. Permission required for outlying Gores Wood

Goodwood Park, Chichester (*Goodwood Estates Co. Ltd*): Outstanding Lebanon cedars, fine oaks, Paulownia, cork oak, limes. Open mostly May-early October

The High Beeches, Handcross (*Hon. E. Boscawen*): Large glades of rare trees, Stuartias, oaks, Brewer spruce, magnolias

Highdown, Goring-by-Sea (*Worthing BC*): Famous chalk garden. Fine maples, cherries, hybrid strawberry-tree, outstanding Chinese hornbeams

Leonardslee, Lower Beeding (*Mr and Mrs R. Loder*): Rare and large trees along 7 km of paths. Drive, rock-garden, long bank, the Dell, Coronation Wood, Mossy Ghyll, Azalea Garden, Pinetum. Outstanding Metasequoias, golden larch, Campbell magnolia, fine coast redwoods, sessile oak, Serbian spruce, Japanese thujas, Ponderosa pine, Himalayan holly. Open daily spring and autumn

Munton House Crematorium (*Worthing BC*): Huge reclining Judas-tree, fine coast redwoods, cypresses, deodars, Morinda spruce

Nymans, Handcross (*NT/The Countess of Rosse*): Outstanding Southern beeches, Eucryphias, rare and tender species in garden. Two pineta, wall-garden, magnolia garden and wilderness. Big Metasequoias. Open daily spring to autumn

St Roche's Arboretum, Singleton (*Mr E. F. W. James*): Large area of remarkable conifers on a chalk slope and some hardwoods. Huge Douglas firs, thujas, coast redwoods, fine Sitka spruce, pines, grand fir, southern beeches, Lucombe oak

Sheffield Park, Uckfield (*NT*): Extensive plantings round three lakes and East Park. Grove of giant sequoias. Conifer Walk, 1910. Outstanding Brewer spruces, Serbian spruce, 150 tupelos (1908 planting), Palm Walk, fine Japanese umbrella pine, Metasequoias, Nikko maples, Montezuma pine, common oaks, pond cypress. Open spring to autumn

Stanmer Park, Brighton (*Public park*): Unique collection of rare elms, unusual maples, limes

Tilgate Park, Crawley (*Crawley BC, Public park*): Mixed old trees; 1966 pinetum. Fine swamp cypresses, keaki, Hondo spruce, dove-tree, Virginia magnolia

Wakehurst Place, Ardingly (*NT*): Huge area, six pineta, Bethlehem Garden, Heather Garden, Japanese Garden, Himalayan Valley, Bloomer's Valley, Mansion Lawn, the Oaks. Outstanding dove-tree, Campbell magnolia, fine rare pines, southern beeches, cider-gums, rare maples, Gowen cypresses, Leyland cypresses, western hemlock, southern catalpa, hickories

West Dean House, Singleton (*The James Trust*): Outstanding horse chestnut, female gingko, fine cedars, oak species

South-west

AVON

Bath Botanic Garden Outstanding Chinese necklace poplar, yellow buckeye, paper-mulberry, golden catalpa, fine Metasequoia, gingkos, silver pendent lime, hornbeam, Balearic box

Henrietta Park, Bath (*Public park*): Outstanding line of seven double horse chestnuts, Lombardy poplar. Good smooth Arizona cypress, gingkos, Tree of Heaven, purple sycamore

Sydney Park, Bath (*Public park*): Notable hybrid catalpa, golden Cappadocian maple, golden poplar, London planes and several beeches

Victoria Park, Bath, (*Public road*): Huge honey-locust, fine

Zelkova, Kentucky coffee-tree. The Dell: Fine conifers; notable
Arizona cypress, gingko, coast redwoods, Cedar of Goa

Blaize Castle, nr Bristol (*Public park*): Big old gingko; Lucombe
oak, Lebanon cedar, Himalayan birch

CORNWALL

Antony House, Torpoint (*NT*): Outstanding cork oak, Japanese
hemlock. Fine gingko, Metasequoia, black walnut, Siebold
hemlock, lacebark pine. Open April-end October

Caerhays Castle, nr Truro (*Mr J. Williams*): Collection of rare
Asiatic oaks unrivalled in variety and size; innumerable other trees
of great rarity. Open occasionally

Glendurgan, Mawnan Smith (*NT*): Fine willow oak, Rauli,
Cunninghamias, Bentham's cornels, western red cedars, Monterey
pines, swamp cypresses. Open March-end October, Mondays,
Wednesdays, Fridays

Lanhydrock, Bodmin (*NT*): Good conifers in old avenue, fine
magnolias, Japanese black pine, Douglas fir; tender trees. Open
daily

Mount Edgcumbe Country Park, Torpoint: Outstanding cork
oak, fine stone pine, Lebanon cedars, gingko. Open daily

Pencarrow, Bodmin (*Sir J. Molesworth-St Aubyn*): Avenue of
1840–1860 conifers, outstanding oriental spruce, Japanese red
cedar, Cunninghamia in America Garden, pinetum, fine monkey-
puzzles, southern beeches, tiger-tail spruce, drooping juniper. Open
daily Easter–October

Trebartha, Launceston (*Mr C. Latham*): Outstanding 50m Sitka
spruce, 46m Norway spruce, fine Oregon maple, noble fir,
European larch, western hemlock, hiba. Open daily

Trelissick, nr Truro (*NT*): Notable Japanese red cedar, Cornish
elms, fine maritime pine, sawara cypress varieties. Open March-end
October, not Sundays

Trengwainton, Penzance (*NT*) Many rare and tender trees.
Notable magnolias, podocarps, eucryphias, myrtles, dove-tree.
Open March–October, not Sundays, Mondays or Tuesdays

Trewithen, Probus (*Mr and Mrs A. M. Galway*): Outstanding rare
maples, birches, southern beeches, dove-tree, Michelia

DEVON

Bicton Gardens (*Lord Clinton*): Very big collection of outsize old conifers and hardwoods; additional 1916 pinetum; many trees added around 1960. Oak collection. Hickories. Open daily

Castlehill, Filleigh (*Lady M. Fortescue*): Outsize Sitka spruce, Douglas firs, Thuja, golden-barred thuja, Lucombe oak, fine Japanese red cedars, grey poplars, western hemlocks, deodar. (Must phone estate office, Filleigh 336)

Cockington Court, Torquay (*Torbay BC Public park*): Large collection hardwoods, conifers (some tender). Notable Kashmir cypress, Metasequoia, Mexican pine, Taiwania, paper birch, roble beech

Coleton Fishacre, Kingswear *(NT):* 1925−40 planting of wide variety of unusual trees. Formosan cypress, Forrest fir. Open Wednesdays, Fridays and Sundays throughout year

Exeter University Campus (*Public roads and gardens of Reed Hall, Streatham Hall):* Outstanding Torreyas, Santa Lucia firs, fine bishop pine, fernleaf oak

Killerton, Silverton *(NT):* Outsize Chinese sweetgum, Monarch birch, quercitron oak, Pacific dogwood, Stuartia. Fine magnolias, incense cedar, thuja, Metasequoia. Open daily

Knightshayes Court, Tiverton *(NT)*: Outstanding Turkey oak, fine Lucombe oak, rare maples, Dombey's beech, giant sequoia, western hemlock, grove of Douglas firs. Open daily April−October

Rosemoor, Great Torrington (*Lady Anne Palmer)*: Great variety of post-1970 rare trees

DORSET

Abbotsbury *(Strangways Estates)*: Outstanding wingnuts, Idesia, Madeira laurel. Many fine tender trees. Magnolias, orange-bark myrtle

Forde Abbey, Chard *(Trustees of Mr G. D. Roper)*: Pagoda-tree, fernleaf beech, wingnut, coast redwood, cedars. Open spring to autumn

Melbury House, nr Yeovil *(Lady Teresa Agnew)*: Outstanding Caucasian wingnut, coast redwood, cypress oak, Grecian fir, Caucasian oak, Monterey cypresses. Open National Gardens days

GLOUCESTERSHIRE

Batsford Arboretum, Moreton-in-the-Marsh *(Lord Dulverton)*: Extensive collection since 1880. New oak collection. Notable oaks, cedars, Metasequoia, Syrian juniper etc. Open April−October

Hester Park, Cheltenham *(Public park)*: Good varied planting 1953; many unusual trees

Lydney Park *(Viscount Bledisloe)*: Outstanding London plane, fine limes. Garden planted 1956, sourgum

Speech House Arboretum, nr Coleford *(FC)*: Large array unusual conifers and hardwoods begun in 1916. Outstanding Cilician fir, Himalayan birch, fine pines, spruces. Always open

Stanway House, nr Broadway *(Lord Neidpath)*: Outstanding Lebanon cedar, Coulter pine; fine oriental plane, oriental spruce, Corsican pine. Open June – August, Wednesdays and Sundays

Westonbirt Arboretum, nr Tetbury *(FC)*: Vast collection, almost continuous planting since 1829. New glades and collections in Silk Wood. Outstanding maples, oaks, birches, limes, hollies. Open daily

SOMERSET

Broadwood, Dunster: Forest road through grove of 1877 Douglas fir to 53m tall and larch, with recent additions

Clapton Court, Crewkerne *(Capt S. Loder)*: Outstanding monster ash, notable Metasequoia, dove-tree. Open daily, except Saturdays

Cricket House Country Park, nr Chard: Good deodars, beech lime

Montacute House, nr Yeovil *(NT)*: Outstanding Monterey cypress, line of 'family circle' regrowth of coast redwood, several giant sequoias

Orchardleigh, Frome: Fine tall Silver pendent lime, incense cedars, coast redwoods, Bhutan pine

WILTSHIRE

Bowood, Calne *(The Earl of Shelburne)*: Outstanding Lebanon cedars, ponderosa pine, hybrid poplars, grove of coast redwoods, fine Morinda spruces, black pines. Atlas cedars, Monterey pine, lodgepole pine. Open spring to autumn

Corsham Court *(Lord Methuen)*: Notable Oriental plane, Lucombe oak, Lebanon cedars, ginkgo, black walnut, Ohio buckeye. Not open Mondays

Longleat *(The Marquess of Bath)*: Pleasure grounds, notable ginkgo, Spanish fir, coast redwood, fine Douglas fir, Brewer spruce. Open daily

Stourhead *(NT)*: Outstanding tulip-tree, tiger-tail spruce,

Macedonian pine. Fine coast redwoods, dove-trees, Japanese white pine, Metasequoias, thuja, noble firs. Open daily

Wilton House *(The Earl of Pembroke)*: Outstanding Lebanon cedars, Golden oak, Lucombe oak, big Bhutan pine, London plane. Open spring to autumn

Eastern England

BEDFORDSHIRE

Woburn Abbey *(Trustees of the Bedford Estates)*: Evergreens, splendid variety of conifers of about 1920 planting, some 1860 conifers. Pleasure Grounds open daily in summer, weekends in winter.

Wrest Park, Silsoe *(DoE):* Notable giant sequoia, Jeffrey pine, Small-leaf limes. Open weekends, April – September

CAMBRIDGESHIRE

Anglesey Abbey, Lode *(NT)*: Extensive planting since 1930; fine Hungarian oak, catalpa. Open Wednesdays – Sundays in summer.

Cambridge University Botanic Garden: Outstanding single-leaf nut-pine, Gerard's pine, pecan, spurleaf, Metasequoia, hybrid catalpa. Open daily

Clare College Gardens, Cambridge: Big Metasequoia, Ohio buckeye. Open daily p.m.

The Fen, Cambridge City *(Public park)*: Fine line Italian alders, huge Lombardy poplars.

HERTFORDSHIRE

Ashridge Park, Berkhamsted *(Management College)*: Fine Blue Algerian cedar, ring of incense cedars, Lobel maples, grand fir. Open April – October, Saturdays and Sundays

Bayfordbury House *(Agricultural College)*: Notable 1760 Lebanon cedars; pinetum with outstanding western larch, fine ponderosa and Crimean pines.

Hatfield House *(The Marquess of Salisbury)*: Some fine old hardwoods; new plantings. Open May – September, not Mondays

LINCOLNSHIRE

Belton Park, Belton *(NT)*: Some fine hardwoods. Silver and sugar maples, sycamores, weeping beech, Trees of Heaven, limes. Open April – October, not Mondays or Tuesdays

Boultham Park, Lincoln *(Public park)*: Outsize 40m railway poplar, Japanese thuja.

Lincoln Arboretum *(Public park)*: Black walnut, wingnut, silver pendent lime.

NORFOLK

Holkham Hall, Wells-next-the-Sea *(The Earl of Leicester)*: Garden with notable snakebark maple, old Corsican pines, fine junipers, tupelos. Open June – September most days

Lyndford Arboretum, Mundford *(FC)*: Large collection 1950 onwards of rare and common conifers and some hardwoods, already fine trees. Notable old Crimean and Corsican pines. Chinese tulip tree, groups of bishop pine, southern beeches. Always open

Sandringham Hall *(HM the Queen)*: Some fine older trees, much recent planting, blue spruce, incense cedar. Open April – September, variously

Talbot Manor, Fincham *(Mr M. Mason)*: Huge variety planted since 1950; notable poplars, alders, beech forms, oaks, maples. Open occasionally

NORTHAMPTONSHIRE

Althorp *(Earl Spencer)*: Arboretum with notable Santa Lucia fir, limber pine, coast redwoods, Likiang spruce, limes, giant sequoias, sweetgums, Dawyck beech, cypress oak, Crimean oak (nr stables). Open daily, p.m.

Castle Ashby *(The Marquis of Northampton)*: Notable horse chestnut, Bhutan pine, Bhutan cypress. Open Sundays April – October

SUFFOLK

Abbey Garden, Bury St Edmunds *(Public park)*: Notable Tree of Heaven, Père David maples, Turkish hazel

East Bergholt Place *(Mrs Maxwell Eley)*: Outstanding rauli; large collection of fine, rare, often tender trees

Hardwick Park, Bury St Edmunds *(Public park)*: Fine cypress oaks, junipers, Algerian firs, Lucombe oak, cedars

Ipswich Arboretum, Christchurch Park *(Public park)*: Cider-gum, alders, willows, big horse chestnut, common oak, white willow

Somerleyton Hall, nr Lowestoft *(Lord and Lady Somerleyton)*: Cider-gum, monkey-puzzles, Monterey pine. Open summer, except Saturdays

Midlands

BUCKINGHAMSHIRE

Ascott House, Wing *(NT)*: Fine colour-planting, golden Atlas cedar; 1897 Jubilee group, paper birch, paperbark maple. Open April – September, Wednesdays and Thursdays

Cliveden, Maidenhead *(NT)*: Outstanding butternut, fine cypress oaks, black locust, blue cedars. Open March – December

Stowe Park *(Stowe School)*: Outstanding Lebanon cedar, good Dawyck beeches, Leyland cypresses, yellow buckeye. Open mid-July – early September, Fridays and weekends

Waddesden, Aylesbury *(NT)*: Fine Arolla pine, noble firs, Grecian fir, small-leaf lime, cedars, ginkgo, oriental spruce, giant sequoias, Chinese privet, silver pendent lime. Open April – October, not Mondays or Tuesdays

CHESHIRE

Granada Arboretum, Jodrell Bank *(University of Manchester)*: Recently established wide selection of hardwoods; notably alders, birches, apples, cherries, Leyland cypresses, limes

Ness/Liverpool University Botanic Garden: Mostly fairly young specimens; notable Paulownia, collection of rowans, flowering trees, pin oak. Open daily

Tatton Park, Knutsford *(NT)*: Chilean incense cedar, fine Metasequoias, Colorado blue spruce, Père David's maple. Open daily

DERBYSHIRE

Chatsworth, Bakewell *(Chatsworth House Trustees)*: Outstanding Weymouth pine, rupelos, sweet chestnut, good pinetum. Open April – October, daily

Elvaston Country Park: Fine junipers, cedars, pines, monkey-puzzles. Open daily

HEREFORDSHIRE & WORCESTERSHIRE

Eastnor Castle, Ledbury *(Mr James Harvey Bathurst)*: Outstanding original blue Atlas cedar, fine pines, incense cedars, rare oaks and conifers over wide area. Tall grand, pindrow and Algerian firs; outstanding bishop pine, Nootka cypresses, Morinda spruces, Turner's oak. Open Sundays spring and summer; Wednesdays, Thursdays, July – August

Hergest Croft, Kington *(R. A. and L. Banks)*: Huge collection, many from original seeds from China; fine and rare conifers, maples, birches. Open daily mid-April to mid-September

Jephson Garden, Leamington Spa *(Public park)*: Fine collection of unusual trees. Notable ginkgo, keaki, catalpas, wingnut, Hungarian and Caucasian oaks, Indian horse chestnut

Queenswood, Hope-under-Dinmore *(Hereford & Worcester CC)*: Varied planting since 1953, many rarities. Open daily

Spetchley Park, Worcester *(Mr and Mrs J. Berkeley)*: Good Zoeschen maple, Serbian spruce, Lucombe oak, 'Aurora' poplar. April – September, not Saturdays

Whitfield, Allensmore *(Mr G. Clive)*: Outstanding sessile oak, weeping oak, ginkgo. Fine 1855 grove of Coast redwoods, giant sequoia. Open occasionally

NOTTINGHAMSHIRE

Clumber Park *(NT)*: Avenue of common lime with one notable broadleaf lime. Fine young pines, Jeffrey, ponderosa, jack pines. Open daily

OXFORDSHIRE

Blenheim Palace, Woodstock *(The Duke of Marlborough)* Notable Lebanon cedar, sugar maple, incense cedars. Open mid-March to end October

Nuneham Arboretum *(University Botanic Garden)*: Fine old conifers, oak, incense cedars; new plantings. Open p.m.

Pusey House, Farringdon *(Mr M. Hornby)*: Notable London place, swamp cypress, Bhutan pine. Open most days April – October

University Botanic Garden, Oxford: Outstanding service trees, green ash, fine ginkgo, black walnut, persimmon. Open daily

University Parks, Oxford *(Public park)*: Notable poplars, pagoda-tree, Turkish hazel, rare thorns

SHROPSHIRE

Hodnet Hall, Market Drayton *(Mr & Mrs A. Heber Percy)*: Fine Metasequoia, Grecian firs, catalpas, dove-trees, cherries, magnolias; fine oaks. Open May – August

Walcot Park *(Mr Parish)*: Original Douglas fir, many fine conifers, Low's fir, hemlocks. Open occasionally

Weston Park, Shifnal *(The Earl of Bradford)*: Outstanding oriental plane, giant sequoia, good Corsican pines, cypress oak. Open summer, daily except Mondays and Fridays

STAFFORDSHIRE

Trentham Park, Stoke-on-Trent *(Public park)*: Unusual hardwoods; yellow buckeyes, trident maple; pinetum, fine Lows and Nikko firs, Japanese thuja, Macedonian pines

Shugborough Park, Stafford *(NT)*: Many fine old trees

Northern England

CUMBRIA

Aira Force, Ullswater *(NT)*: Notable Sitka spruce, Himalayan fir, Bhutan cypress, Norway spruce, grand fir

Fallbarrow Park, Bowness-on-Windermere *(Public park)*: Fine conifers, deodar, Morinda spruce, mountain hemlock, Bhutan pine

Holker Hall, Cark-in-Cartmel *(Mr H. Cavendish)*: Probable original monkey-puzzle, outstanding Hungarian and Mirbeck oaks, fine Hupeh crab, sourgum, ginkgo. Open April – October, not Saturdays

Hutton-in-the-Forest, Penrith *(Lord Inglewood)*: Outstanding giant sequoia, Low's fir, hornbeam, fine Sitka spruce, elms. Always open

Lingholm, Derwentwater *(Viscount Rochdale)*: Outstanding Norway pruce, fine Scots pines, giant sequoia, silver firs, cucumber-tree. Open April – October, weekdays

Monk Coniston, Coniston *(The Holiday Fellowship)*: Outstanding pindrow fir, Douglas fir, Sitka spruce, Japanese red cedar, fine old larches. By permission

Muncaster Castle *(Sir W. Pennington Ramsden Bt)*: Outstanding Dombey beeches, rauli, fine coast redwoods, noble firs, Leyland cypress. Daily except Mondays

Skelgill Wood, Ambleside *(NT)*: Beside Stagshaw Garden. A few superb conifers, grand firs, Douglas fir to over 50m, Hondo spruce

Wray Castle *(NT)*: Fine big coast redwood, giant sequoia, Thujopsis, monkey-puzzle, Douglas fir, Atlas cedar, fernleaf beech

MERSEYSIDE

Calderstones Park, Mossley Hill, Liverpool *(Public park)*: Wide selection; notable rowan, apple, cherry glades; avenue of American lime; notable Italian alder

NORTHUMBERLAND

Beaufront Castle, Hexham *(Mr A. Cuthbert)*: Outstanding beech, cutleaf lime, Likiang spruce. Pinetum with fine foxtail pine and other rarities. Open occasionally

Cragside, Rothbury *(NT)*: Many huge conifers; notable 46m Low's firs, Douglas firs, western hemlocks, red fir. Open April-September daily; October-March week-ends

Howick Gardens, Craster *(The Howick Trustees Ltd)*: Fine maples, birches, katsuratrees, Hungarian oak

NORTH YORKSHIRE

Castle Howard *(Lord Howard of Henderskelfe)*: Old hardwoods and vast new collection of unusual, rare and very rare trees, as comprehensive as any, with recent cultivars 1975 on. (1978 arboretum not currently open.) Open daily April – October

Harlow Carr, Ripon *(Northern Horticultural Society)*: Fairly recent wide collection. Open daily

Studley Royal/Fountains Abbey *(NT and North Yorkshire CC)*: Outstanding wild cherry, sweet chestnuts, fine oaks, sycamores, a few big conifers

Thorpe Perrow, Bedale *(Sir J. and Lady Ropner)*: Enormous collection, 1880 with 1930 colour glades, collections of rare and notable maples, cherries, oaks, beech poplars, spruces, pines, white beams, rowans, crabs, laburnums, thorns etc. Outstanding line of rare limes; many pillar apples. Open April – October

Wales

CLWYD

Gwysany, Wrexham *(Mr P. Davies-Cook)*: Lines of old conifers being landscaped with young trees. Open occasionally

GWYNEDD

Bodnant Garden, Tal-y-Cafn *(NT)*: Huge collection with outstanding Grecian, Low's and grand firs, weeping giant sequoia, western hemlocks, Chinese hemlock, Mexican white pines, coast redwood, magnolias, maples, tender species. Mid-March – mid-October

Penrhyn Castle, Bangor *(NT)*: Umbrella pines, Metasequoia, Winter's Bark, Sequoias, Ecryphias, Ginkgo, Styrax. Open spring to autumn, daily except Tuesdays

POWYS

Leighton Arboretum *(Royal Forestry Society)*: Grove of 1857 redwoods, original 'Leighton Green' Leyland cypress, big Morinda spruce, Japanese red cedar, medium age and recent pinetum. Open daily

Powis Castle *(Earl Powis/NT)*: Outstanding oaks, ponderosa pine, giant sequoia, Douglas firs. Fine coast red woods, silver firs, maples, ginkgo, dove-tree. Gardens, open daily p.m. Park open daily

The Gliffaes Hotel, nr Crickhowell *(Mr and Mrs Brabner)*: Outstanding Japanese red cedar, fine yellow buckeyes, giant sequoias, coast redwood, Metasequoia, Lucombe oak

SOUTH GLAMORGAN

Cathays Park, Cardiff *(Public park)*: Good ginkgos, Leyland cypress, beech

Dyffryn Gardens, St Nicholas *(Public park)*: Huge variety of fine and rare trees. Outstanding paperbark maples, Brewer spruces, Chinese wingnut, Chinese elm, tupelo, many oaks, birches, maples, southern beeches

Roath Park, Cardiff *(Public park)*: Pagoda-tree, ginkgo, black walnut, paperback maple

WEST GLAMORGAN

Clyne Castle, Swansea *(Public park)*: Fine winter's bark, bigleaf storax, Cunninghamia

Margam Abbey *(Swansea/West Glamorgan CC)*: Fine fernleaf beech, bay laurels, old tulip-trees, oriental plane, Cedar of Goa. Open April – October, not Mondays

Singleton Abbey, Swansea *(Public park)*: Laurelia, rare wing-nut, Metasequoia, Italian cypresses, Montpelier maple, Idesia

Northern Ireland
ARMAGH

Gosford Castle, Markethill *(Forestry Department)*: Outstanding Himalayan fir, noble fir, fine redwoods, cypresses. Open daily

DOWN

Bangor Castle *(Public park)*: Fine blue gums, Santa Lucia and noble firs, bishop and Monterey pines

Castlewellan, nr Newcastle *(Forestry Department)*: Extensive and expanding collection with many huge old conifers, rare and tender species. Outstanding Algerian fir, Brewer spruce, California nutmeg, eucalypts; fine Himalayan hemlock, New Zealand red beech, Japanese thuja, junipers. Morinda spruce, Himalayan fir, cypresses. Open daily

Mount Stewart, Portaferry *(NT)*: Large gardens with big blue gums and other eucalypts, redwoods, King Boris fir, Kashmir and Monterey cypresses, outstanding Monterey pines and many rare, tender trees

Rowalline, Saintfield *(NT)*: Remarkable collection of southern beeches, big monkey-puzzles, fine bishop and Macedonian pines, Likiang and Brewer spruces, dove-tree, Paulownia. Open daily except weekends in winter

Tullymore Castle *(Forestry Department)*: 'Seven Sisters', very big old silver firs, notable Grecian fir, deodars, Monterey pine, Japanese white pine, willow podocarp, Japanese thuja, tulip-tree. Open daily

TYRONE

Drum Manor, Cookstown *(Forestry Department)*: Outstanding western hemlock, Himalayan fir, noble fir, fine redwoods, cypresses. Open daily

The Irish Republic

CORK

Annes Grove, Castletownroche: Notable willow podocarp, Cornish elms. Open Easter to end September, not Saturdays

Ashbourne House Hotel, nr Fota: Notable Kashmir Cypress, gingko, dove-tree, katsura-tree, blue gum, roble beech, souroum, California horse chestnut

Fota, Carigtwohill *(University College Cork)*: Outstanding Himalayan cypress, Japanese red Korean cedars, Torreya, notable grand fir, sorrel tree, Hungarian oak and several great rarities. Open April-end September

Ilnacullin, Garinish, Glengarriff (by boat) *(Comm. Public Works)*: Renowned collection of plants from southern hemisphere, mainly 1910–1940. Notable Mexican pine, Japanese black pine, Totara. Open March-October

DUBLIN

Glasnevin Botanic Garden (*Dept Agriculture*): Notable poplars, Algerian fir, several willows, good collection of pines, cypresses, maples, oaks, spruces. Fine Zelkova, Suttner's plane, Serbian spruce. Open daily

KERRY

Derreen, Kenmare (*Hon David Bigham*): Outstanding Monterey cypress, Monterey pine, Pacific fir, Japanese red cedars, blue gums, Lawson 'Erecta' and 'Gracilis Pendula'. Open April – September, Sundays, Tuesdays and Thursdays

Dunloe Castle Hotel: Outstanding varigated table-dogwood, Stroll's maple, fine Wissel cypress, paperback maple, Mexican and bishop pines, Taiwania, crested beech, rare limes, Zoeschen maple

LAOIS

Abbeyleix (*de Vesci Estates*): Original David Douglas Sitka spruce, notable silver firs and spruces in variety, Bhutan pine, Japanese larch, Zoeschen maple, single-leaf ash. Open Easter – end September

LIMERICK

Currah Chase, Adare (*Forestry and Wildlife Service*): Big silver fir, monkey-puzzle, Monterey cypress, Monterey pine, European larch, Bhutan pine, manna ash. Open daily

OFFALY

Birr Castle, Birr (*The Earl and Countess of Rosse*): Extensive collections of Asiatic conifers, maples and others, mostly from original seed. Outstanding Macnab cypress, drooping juniper, hybrid wingnut, grey poplar, Henry's lime. Open daily

WATERFORD

Curraghmore (*The Marquis of Waterford*): Original David Douglas Sitka spruce and grand fir. Outstanding giant sequoias, Mexican white pine, Caucasian fir, Japanese red cedars, coast redwood. Open April-September, Thursdays only

WEXFORD

John F. Kennedy Arboretum, New Ross (*Forestry and Wildlife Service*): Extensive plantings, species collections and plots begun in 1960. Notable Eucalypts. Open daily

Avondale Forest Garden, Rathdrum (*Forestry and Wildlife Service*): Outstanding Wissel and Arizona cypresses, Veitch's silver fir, three old common silver firs, Macedonian and western white pine. 1904 plots. Many fine eucalypts. Open daily

Powerscourt, Enniskerry (*Mrs Slazenger*): Large area of huge trees. Outstanding blue gums, monkey-puzzles, Mexican pine, Coulter pine, Likiang spruce, dragon spruce, Himalayan fir, winter's bark. Open Easter – end October

Mount Usher, Ashford (*Mrs Jaye*): Outstanding Dombey southern beeches, eucalypts, Canary pine, Chinese firs, Montezuma pines, rare maples and birches, Tasmanian cedars. Open mid-March – end September

Scotland

Borders Region

Dawyck Arboretum, Peebles (*Royal Botanic Garden*): Huge collection with many outstanding Asiatic silver firs and spruces, maples; original Dawyck beech, fine Brewer spruces, Douglas firs. Open daily April–September

Dryburgh Abbey, Selkirk (*Scottish Dept*): Fine Cedars of Lebanon, deodar, Altlas cedar, big common lime, Low's fir. Open daily

Dryburgh Abbey Hotel (*adjacent to Abbey*): Outstanding fastigiate Scots pine, big Chinese jumper

Kailzie Gardens, Peebles (*Mrs A. M. Richard*): Fine 1725 larches, sugar maple, wych elms. Open daily March – October

The Monteviot Pinery, Jedburgh (*The Marquis of Lothiam*): Notable Macedonian pine, Sitka spruce, variegated oak, Hungarian oak, mountain hemlocks. Open daily

Central Region

Culcleuch Castle, Fintry (*Baron Hercules Robinson*): Outstanding Grecian firs, Sitka spruces, single-leaf ash, fine Jeffrey, ponderosa, lodgepole and Crimean pines, Hungarian oak. Open daily

Gargunnock (*Miss V. Stirling*): Line of fine giant sequoias, outstanding common oak in field, fernleaf beech behind house. Open at times

Stirling University Campus, Airthrie Castle: Outstanding giant sequoias, line of fine incense cedars, Arolla pine

Dumfries and Galloway

Castle Kennedy, Stranraer (*The Earl and Countess of Stair*): Fine avenues of monkey-puzzle, bishop pine, cider-gums, thuja, Monterey pines. Open daily April – September.

Drumlanrig Castle, Thornhill (*The Duke of Buccleuch*): Original Douglas fir, fine silver fir, old larch, Eugene poplar, biggest sycamore. Open May – August, not Fridays

Glenlee Park, New Galloway (*Mr Agnew*): Outstanding Douglas firs, giant sequoia, larch, Norway spruce, all 40 – 55m tall. Open occasionally

Threave Garden, Castle Douglas (*NTS*): Large and varied recent planting, fine alders, poplars, pines, maples, cherries. Open daily

Grampian Region

Balmoral Castle (*HM the Queen*): Fine Low's and red firs, many good noble firs, Douglas firs, western hemlocks, small younger pinetum. Open May – July

Blairquhan, Straiton (*Mr John Hunter-Blair*): Orchard of huge conifers; notable jack pine, shore pine, rare spruces. Maria's Walk and two mile drive of fine silver firs, spruces, hemlocks of mixed ages. Vast beech above house.

Crathes Castle, Banchory (*NTS*): Fine Douglas fir, deodar, outstanding rare Zelkova, good Brewer spruce, Taiwania, madrone, Tibetan cherry. Open daily

Culzean Castle, Maybole (*NTS*): Fine Montezuma pine, red fir (Happy Valley), Monterey pines, two big Sitka spruces, Crimean and Scots pines. Hybrid catalpa (Wall Garden), fifty Chusan palms, Katsura trees, three wingnuts. Open daily

Drum Castle, Aberdeen (*NTS*): Delavay fir, smooth Arizona cypress, Jeffrey hemlock, Brewer spruce, Chinese necklace poplar, yellow buckeye. Open May – September

Haddo House, Methlick (*NTS*): Two original giant sequoia, notable beech

Innes House, Llanbryde (*Mr Iain Tennant*): Outstanding larch, Lucombe oak, madrone, many unusual species for the region. Open some days

Highland Region

Ardineisaig Hotel, Tyanuilt: Outstanding noble and Caucasian firs, monkey-puzzle, Sitka spruce, Douglas fir, southern beeches, Chinese beech

Brodick Castle, Arran (*NTS*): Numerous huge old conifers and many tender evergreen broadleaves. Notable rauli, eucalypts, sassafras

Cawdor Castle (*The Earl of Cawdor*): Outstanding Low's fir, western hemlock, Doulgas fir, fine horse chestnut, coast redwoods, noble fir, Giant Sequoias. Open May – September

Crarae Garden, Furnace (*Sir Ilay Campbell Bt*): Notable eucalypts, tender broadleaves and rare conifers, Kawakami fir, Cunninghamia, sugar pine, cypresses. Open March – October

Inveraray Castle (*The Duke of Argyll*): Notable grand firs, deodars, larch, weeping sequoia, Leyland cypress (Frews Bridge), cucumber tree. Open April – October variously

Kilmun Forest Garden, nr Dunoon (*FC*): Hillside of plots and specimens of rare and unusual conifers and broadleaves, notable eucalypts; post 1950. Always open

Moniac Glen, nr Beauly (*FC*): Tallest Douglas fir stand in Britain, 1880, to 60m; grand fir 55m; big incense cedar, silver fir, Lawson cypress. Always open

Stonefield Castle Hotel, Tarbett: Remarkable clubmoss cypress, King Boris fir, fine Sawara cypress forms, willow podocarp, Himalayan hemlock

Strone House Arboretum, Cairndow, Arrochar (*Lady Glenkinglas*): Tallest tree in Britain (grand fir 60m) outstanding thujas, Fitzroya, Sawara cypresses, immense common silver fir, fine larch, oriental spruce, mountain hemlock, Hinoki cypress. Open daily

Younger Botanic Garden, Benmore, Dunoon (*Royal Botanic Garden, Edinburgh*): Towering 55m Douglas firs everywhere; avenue of giant sequoias to 50m; Sitka sprue and western hemlock to 50m; outstanding Pacific fir, Forrest fir, rauli, roble beeches, Hondo spruce; Nordmann firs to 48m. Open April – October

Lothian

Royal Botanic Garden, Edinburgh (*Ministry of Agriculture*): Outstanding Van Volxem maple, golden beech, Likiang spruce; big collections oaks, maples, birches, pines and rarities. Open daily

Smeaton House, East Linton (*Mr and Mrs G. G. Gray*): Extensive collection. Notable Italian alder, Pindrow fir, roundleaf beech, original sequoias, a gutta-percha tree. Open at times

Tyninghame, East Linton (*Earl of Haddington*): Outstanding Bosnian pine, Crimean pine. Fine Hers's maples, Cornish elm, katsura-tree, beeches. Open June – September

Tayside

Blair Castle, Blair Atholl (*The Duke of Atholl*): Diana's Grove, grand firs, 50 – 55m, noble firs to 46m, Douglas firs to 55m, outstanding Japanese larch, red fir, Low's fir. Open April – October

Glamis Castle (*The Earl of Strathmore and Kinghorne*): Policies; notable grand firs, hybrid larch, noble fir, thujas. Pinetum nearby, notable Nikko fir, oriental spruces. Open May – September

The Hermitage, Invet (*NTS*): Group of big Douglas firs, a common silver fir, view of 60m Douglas across the river.

Scone Palace Pinetum (*Earl of Mansfield*): Square of four immense 1851 Sitka spruces, lines of 1866 mixed conifers, outstanding giant sequoia, western hemlock, Jeffrey pine, noble firs. Open May – mid-October

Index

Leyland (*Cupressocyparis leylandii*) 94, **95**, 128
  'Castwellan Gold' 94
  'Haggerston Grey' 94, **95**
  'Leighton Green' 94, **95**
Nootka (*Chamaecyparis notkatensis*) 94, 95
Smooth Arizona (*C. glabra*) 128
Swamp/Bald (*Taxodium distichum*) 102, **103**

Dove Tree (*Davidia involucrata*) 128

Elm (*Elmus*) 34–7
  Dutch (*Ulmus* x *hollandica* 'Hollandica') 36
  English (*U. procera*) 34, **35**
  Huntingdon (*Ulmus* x *hollandica* 'Vegeta') 36–7
  Smoothleaf (*U. carpinifolia*) 35
  White (*U. laevis*) 37
  Wych (*U. glabra*) 36, **37**
Eucalyptus (*Eucalyptus*) *see* Gum

Fig (*Ficus carica*) 42
Fir, Douglas (*Pseudotsuga menziesii*) 108–9
Fir, Silver (*Abies*) 104–7
  Caucasian (*A. nordmanniana*) **104**, 105
  European Silver Fir (*A. alba*) 105, **105**
  Grand (*A. grandis*) 106, 128
  Korean (*A. koreana*) 107, 128
  Noble (*A. procera*) 106, 107; var. *glauca* 106

Ginkgo *see* Maidenhair tree (*Ginkgo biloba*)
Gum (*Eucalyptus*) 80–1
  Blue (*E. globulus*) 80
  Cider (*E. gunnii*) 80–1, 128
  Snow (*E. niphophila*) 128

Hawthorn (*Crataegus*) 48–9
  Hawthorn/May (*C. monogyna*) 48, **49**
  Midland Thorn (*C. oxycantha/ C. laevigata*) 48
  Plumleaf (*Crataegus* x *prunifolia*) 48–9
Hazel (*Corylus avellana*) 24–5
  Turkish (*C. colurna*) 128

Hemlock (*Tsuga*) 116–17
  Eastern (*T. canadensis*) **116**, 117
  Mountain (*T. mertensiana*) 129
  Western (*T. heterophylla*) 116, **117**, 129
Holly (*Ilex*) 70–1
  Common (*I. aquifolium*) 70, **71**
    'Golden Milkmaid' 70, **71**
    Handsworth New Silver 70
    Hedgehog ('Ferox') 70, **71**
    Laurel-leaf ('Laurifolia') 70
  Highclere (*Ilex* x *altaclerensis*) 70–1
    'Golden King' 71
    'Hendersonii' 71
    'Hodginsii' 71
    'Wilsonii' 71
  Madeira (*I. perado*) 70
Honeylocust (*Gleditsia triacanthos*) 68, **69**, 129
Hornbeam (*Carpinus*) 24–5
  Common (*C. betulus*) 24, **25**
  European hop- (*Ostrya carpinifolia*) 24, **25**

Indian Bean Tree *see* Catalpa

Judas Tree (*Cercis siliquastrum*) 68, 129
Juniper (*Juniperus*) 96–7
  Chinese (*J. chinensis*) 96–7
  Common (*J. communis*) 96, **97**
  Dwarf (var. *nana*) 96, **97**
  Golden Chinese ('Aurea') **96**, 97
  Irish ('Hibernica') 96
  Swedish ('Suecica') 96
  Meyer's Blue (*J. squamata* 'Meyeri') 97

Katsura Tree (*Cercidiphyllum japonicum*) 129
Keaki (*Zelkova serrata*) *see under* Zelkova

Laburnum (*Laburnum*) 66
  Common (*L. anagyroides*) 66
  Scotch (*L. alpinum*) 66
  Voss's (*Laburnum* x *watereri* 'Vossii') 66, 129
Larch (*Larix*) 112–13
  European (*L. decidua*) 112, **113**, 129
  Hybrid (*Larix* x *eurolepsis*)

RSNC

The Royal Society for Nature Conservation is pleased to endorse these excellent, fully illustrated pocket guide books which provide invaluable information on the wildlife of Britain and Northern Europe. Royalties from each book sold will go to help the RSNC's network of 48 Wildlife Trusts and over 50 Urban Wildlife Groups, all working to protect rare and endangered wildlife and threatened habitats. The RSNC and the Wildlife Trusts have a combined membership of 184,000 and look after over 1,800 nature reserves. If you would like to find out more, please contact the RSNC, The Green, Nettleham, Lincoln, LN2 2NR. Telephone 0522 752326.